L4 HOUSE / LUCIANO KRUK

WE WANTED THE HOUSE

TO LIE AMID THE WOODS

MASTERPIECE
SERIES

L4 HOUSE / LUCIANO KRUK

INTRODUCTION BY CAROLINA QUIROGA | EPILOGUE BY EKATERINA KUNZEL

COMPLETED BUILDING PHOTOGRAPHY BY DANIELA MAC ADDEN | AERIAL PHOTOS BY DIEGO MEDINA

OSCAR RIERA OJEDA
PUBLISHERS

CONTENTS

INTRODUCTION

BY CAROLINA QUIROGA

L4 HOUSE
COSTA ESMERALDA, BUENOS AIRES

"A house is more than just a building: it is a tool of human life, because a house it is related to that life, and because there is something deeply vital that is inseparable from its intimate structure and that evidences how different it is from a common object. It is the result of a series of converging factors that determine it: a house's definition cannot be apart from the sensitivity underlying its configuration" (Sacriste, 1990).

L4 House has that profoundly honest architecture in which the building speaks on its own, with no need of a narrative to be understood, and it is this that defines one of its fundamental values. However, as Sacriste points out, there are underlying aspects that support and give meaning to the reflective and creative processes behind doing architecture that can be thoroughly thought about.

This foreword aims at understanding L4 within a set of key characteristics that define its author's work. But it is also an invitation to reveal how he sees reality and, to make it possible, concepts in this book are accompanied and illustrated by his own records, images, stories, processes and references. Summing up, this introduction attempts to throw light over a universe that is perhaps hidden at one's first approach to every work of architecture.

Houses as an Essential Topic

The first question in L4 is that it expresses one of the distinct features of Luciano Kruk's search: houses as an essential topic in the field of architecture. To make a house and even to achieve the appropriate results does not necessarily imply exploring a state of the art. To Kruk, instead, this program represents an act of commitment towards the basic cell that defines living and the chance to assume the professional exercise from its capacity to transform and improve the spaces where domestic life occurs.

L4 is not an isolated act: it belongs to a series of individual houses developed by his current studio—Luciano Kruk Ar-

CAROLINA QUIROGA Architect and Specialist Heritage Conservation and Reuse FADU, UBA. Professor and researcher in the field of architectural design and heritage interventions in the Faculty of Architecture, Design and Urbanism of the University of Buenos Aires, Argentina and the University of Belgrano, Buenos Aires, Argentina. Author of publications and presentations at local and international level. Member of ICOMOS (International Council on Monuments and Sites), Paris, France and DOCOMOMO (International Commitee for Documentation and Conservation of Buildings, Sites and Neighbourhoods of the Modern Movement), Lisboa, Portugal. Collaborator of the Rotterdam Woont Foundation, the Netherlands.

SESC Pompéia, São Paulo, Brazil, by Lina Bo Bardi (top left and above).

Jaragua Apartment Building, São Paulo, Brazil, by Paulo Mendes Da Rocha (above).

quitectos (2012 to this day)—and by BAK studio—Besonías, Almeida, Kruk (2000-2012). In these houses, the relationships among site, usage, shape, and matter have been studied with great rigor and precision as well as with great sensitivity. Other scales and programs, such as housing complexes within the urban fabric, have been tackled with the same conceptual and constructive quality.

The house that motivates this publication shows the influence in Kruk's work of Modern Movement Architecture—Le Corbusier, Mies van der Rohe, Alvar Aalto and Aino Marsio Aalto. It also evidences the influence of the adaptation processes of these universal ideas into our Latin American context: Eduardo Sacriste, Horacio Baliero, Carmen Córdova, and Mario Roberto Alvarez in Argentina and Lina bo Bardi, João Batista Vilanova Artigas and Oscar Niemeyer in Brazil, among others. Likewise, it expresses the influence of figures such as Paulo Mendes da Rocha.

The series of drawings that develops the study of L4's equipment and furniture shows an integral design approach to the house's topic. Evoking Charlotte Perriand's sketches, these diagrams display a remarkably thorough exploration of elements, details and fixings. At the same time, each piece relates to the building's general set up and makes it difficult to imagine the whole and the part as two separate entities.

Architecture and landscape

Its relationship with the surrounding environment is another relevant aspect in L4. On the one side, without emulating nature or pretending to integrate with it mimetically, the building stands as the product of human inventiveness. The purity with which its volume was designed and the use of glass and concrete as the main materials evidence how differentiation became a statement. On the other side, there is a series of formal and spatial strategies that produce a strong integration between architecture and landscape. Both features come together to establish a constant dialogue between artifice and nature.

Huge piled rocks in the landscape become a metaphor that summarizes the author's philosophy. This is the image with which Kruk opens many of his conferences, pointing out that

Museu Brasileiro de Escultura (MuBE), São Paulo, Brazil, by Paulo Mendes Da Rocha (above). Plains of the Pampas, Buenos Aires Province, Argentina (below).

architecture is essentially building, building something that shelters and protects with the minimum available resources, and it is in this essential action that resides the beauty of architecture. Likewise, he states that not only does this construction made of rocks use elements of the landscape, it also ultimately becomes a part of it.

Territories and landscapes support architecture and, at the same time, inspire it. We can mention some of the elements in the seaside landscape of the Buenos Aires Province—Pinamar, Villa Gesell—where he built some summer houses: the sea, the dunes, the pinewoods. We can also name memories and images captured during travels and trips throughout different regions in Argentina and South America: the Patagonian steppe, the infinite horizon of the Pampas, or the cultural paths of Peru, among others.

Kruk sees landscape as a contemplation experience and as an esthetic category, as it is expressed in some shots of director Carlos Sorín's movie Intimate Stories, yet another of his references. The enhancement and the contemplation of the landscape become apparent in L4: the volume's implantation in the middle of the woods, prompting the need to go through a path to enter the house; the decision to locate the social areas of the program at an intermediate level, achieving the best sights; and the careful set of the framings,

Costa Esmeralda's beach, Buenos Aires Province, Argentina (above and opposite page top left). San Martin Park, Mendoza, Argentina (opposite page bottom left).

avoiding barriers that interfere in the relationship with the outside. Even more significantly, this idea of appreciating the surroundings and interacting with them is expressed in the exploitation of the terrace, which lodges areas—swimming pool, solarium—that are in direct relationship with nature.

[Im] Material

A big part of the effort in L4's design is oriented towards architecture's material dimension. However unavoidable an issue it might be, and architecture as a discipline reflects specifically on the act of building, Kruk considers it to be a substantial variable that stands out from the beginning of the design process. As expressed by his sketches, right from the first lines, each concept translates into a consequent exercise with its intrinsic notion of materiality that is later deepened and adjusted.

One characteristic of the project is that it does not just explore the boring of the solid or the substitution of opaque elements by transparent ones, it also explores the immaterial elements that define the architectonic space: light, shadows, voids, time. Paradoxically, the immaterial is a projecting material that must to be manipulated, experimented on, and articulated instead of being conceived as a resulting product. In that same sense, and L4 not being a permanent residence—which hinders its care in a natural area as that of Costa Esmeralda—, concrete was chosen for the house due to its low maintenance need and for its expressive and plastic capacity to be molded.

L4's paths, transitions, and spatial articulation crystallize the purpose of a statement born to be materialized. Rationality and technical practicality go hand in hand with the search for atectonicity, transgression, dissolution, and tension. The material and the immaterial combine together into an austere, silent and subtle space that stimulates the senses without stridency as very few works of architecture do.

Ekaterina Kunzel, who integrates the design team, chooses these words as a synthesis to this philosophy: "If a work of architecture consists of forms and contents which combine to create a strong fundamental mood that is powerful enough to affect us, it may possess the qualities of a work of art. This art has, however, nothing to do with interesting configurations or originality. It is concerned with insights and understanding, and above all with truth. Perhaps poetry is an unexpected truth." (Zumthor, 1992).

Reality and poetry

A pragmatism that carries an immense sensitivity define this house: reality and poetry. We are going through a time when current architectural production enshrines spectacular shapes and icons void of content, and, in the opposite way, praises the precarious. In this context of confusion, a house

like L4 signifies a reconnection to those basic activities that dignify the architect's profession: to draw ideas, and to draw them once again, to think about construction processes and buildings' maintenance, to pay attention to detail.

Maybe this distance from shallowness and what is ephemeral will make this house transcend its time. Academically, its sincerity carries a didactic capacity that teaches that shape is the result of procedures and methods oriented by an attitude towards design: it should be mentioned that reference to Kruk's work is common in schools of architecture. Regarding to the exercise of the profession, L4 collaborates in the current necessary debates, and in those that will come, about the ethic and esthetic sense in architectural production. Thus, I dare say that L4's message is just starting, and that new interpretations, meanings, and questions about this house will come up in the future.

August 2016

References

Sacriste, Eduardo, Sobre casas y templos, Volume 13 in the series "Ediciones previas", Secretaria de Extensión Universitaria, Facultad de Arquitectura, Diseño y Urbanismo, Universidad de Buenos Aires, Argentina, 1990.

Zumthor, Peter, Pensar la arquitectura, Editorial Gustavo Gili, Barcelona, Spain, 1992.

Tandil's stony landscape and mountainious range, Buenos Aires Province, Argentina (above). Patagonia's lake, Argentina (below).

DESIGN

DESCRIPTION

After building several houses in Costa Esmeralda, and captivated as we were by the place, my girlfriend Ekaterina and I set up to project one for ourselves there. We wanted a house where we could stay for short periods of time, suitable for having friends over and, eventually, for rental.

Costa Esmeralda is located thirteen kilometers north off the city of Pinamar and four hours away from Buenos Aires. Barrio Marítimo II, where the plot of land is located, is set parallel to the sea. A screen of pines lies between the neighborhood and the seacoast, thus respecting the 200 meter setback required by provincial regulations.

Lines of maritime pines occupied the lot, an almost virgin sand dune. Regarding the terrain's topography, while there is a two meters slope from side to side, it descends longitudinally in a soft slant toward the sea.

Two were the reasons for choosing the materiality. On the one side, having built other houses in exposed concrete, we knew this material stays in good conditions for a long time practically with no maintenance. On the other, we thought its color and texture would establish a harmonious dialogue with the place's natural surroundings.

Widespread, bright and intimately related to the outside, the social area should be the most important part of the house; the private area should comprise four bedrooms, as independent from one another as possible, each of them with its own bathroom. We aimed at developing most of the plan in a single level and at having a greater outdoor area in a higher level, where water should be present and where we could contemplate the striking natural environment from. We agreed that the trees and the terrain's particular topography were jewels the architectural project should respect.

We wanted the house to lie amid the woods, surrounded by the place's immanent atmosphere. That is why we decided to set the house back into the lot more than the minimum distances required by regulations. While setting the house back away from the street would give more privacy to the interior, the rear would not suffer any harm due to the fact that it expands visually beyond the limits of the terrain and merges into the pine woods next to the sea.

Aiming at producing some contrast for the senses, to enter the house one must go from a gloomy semi covered space, through a narrow staircase enclosed by blind exposed concrete walls and, finally, into an open bright area: the main floor.

Regarding the main floor's design, in order to give every room as much privacy as possible, each one was located in a corner of this quadrangular floorplan. The central hall would house the social activities. Helping to organize this area, a stairway going up to the rooftop lies at the heart of the floorplan and gives order to the space as it separates the kitchen and dining area on one side, and the living room on the other.

The bedrooms' –and their bathrooms'– equipment was detached from the house's outline, thus freeing its supporting walls.

On the topographically highest side, where the main floor's platform stands on the natural ground, the side wall was reduced to a hanging partition opening the interior to the outside through a longitudinal lower crack that protects the inner space from the looks of the neighboring lot. On the lowest side,

in which the house hangs two meters above the natural terrain, a low wall with a high longitudinal opening constituted the outline. Both solutions allowed for outdoor visuals and spaces full of natural light, without losing the inside's privacy.

While the sides were closed by blind walls with horizontal cracks, both the front and the rear were enclosed by a transparent barrier occupying the box's whole width and height that directs the views and frames the visuals. On the rear, the opening framings help the inside expand into the semi covered deck and merge into the outdoor space.

The concrete's own malleability allowed the stairs to be conceived as an autonomous sculptural element. The walls that separate the bedrooms from the central area were treated with the same expressive plasticity, thus generating niches and protruding volumes that function as fixed furniture.

With regards to the house's illumination and given the floorplan's depth, it was decided that the natural lighting would be reinforced from the rooftop. The crystal box containing the stairs bathes the social area's center in sunlight. Linear cracks were incorporated into the inner partitions that limit the kitchen-dining sector in search of different natural light effects throughout the day on their surface. Also, the bathrooms were illuminated by means of skylights placed over the showers.

A big slab sustained by an inverted beams system, supported by partitions inside the floorplan, and metal columns disposed on the side limits as parts of the aluminum framings compose

the supporting structure. In order to emphasize the house's horizontality and to diminish the beams structural system's visual impact, it was set back from the exterior enclosures, thus generating cantilevers that function as brise-soleils.

Embraced by the pines' canopies, a peaceful contemplation space unfolds on the rooftop. Due to the transparency of the box containing the stairs, views in all directions can be experienced. Covered by a wooden deck and furnished by a shower area and two adjacent swimming pools, this viewing space is enriched by the sight of the sea.

We built a box amid a slice of nature and, by letting the exterior flow in and out through it, we made it a constituent part of its environment. Thus, the box and its surroundings merge and vibrate in consonant harmony. Through its spatial synthesis and the simple character of its materiality, we intended the house to wake its inhabitants' perceptions and to maximize their senses, as in the mystic reciprocity the often appears between people and things.

SKETCHES

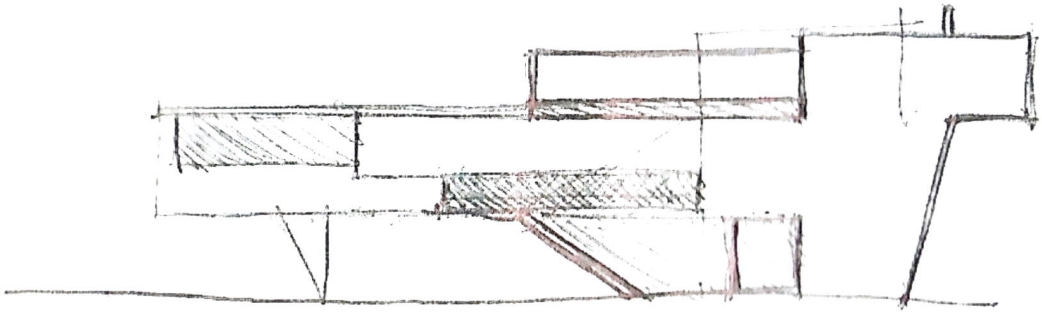

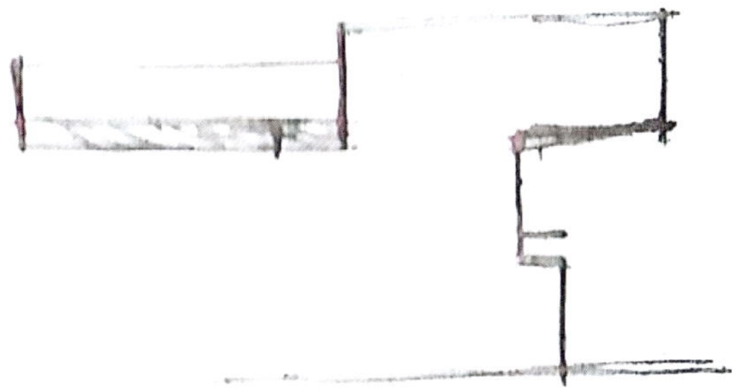

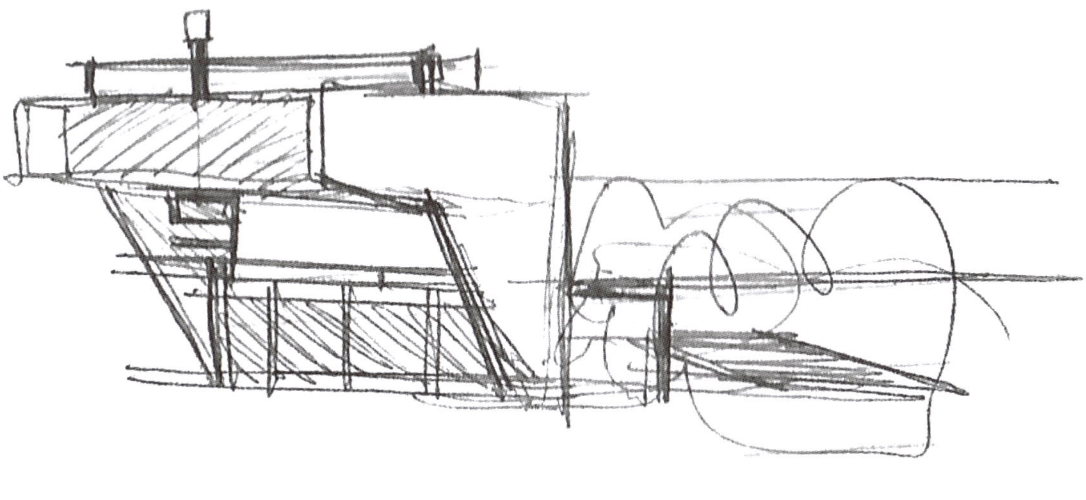

Early house version

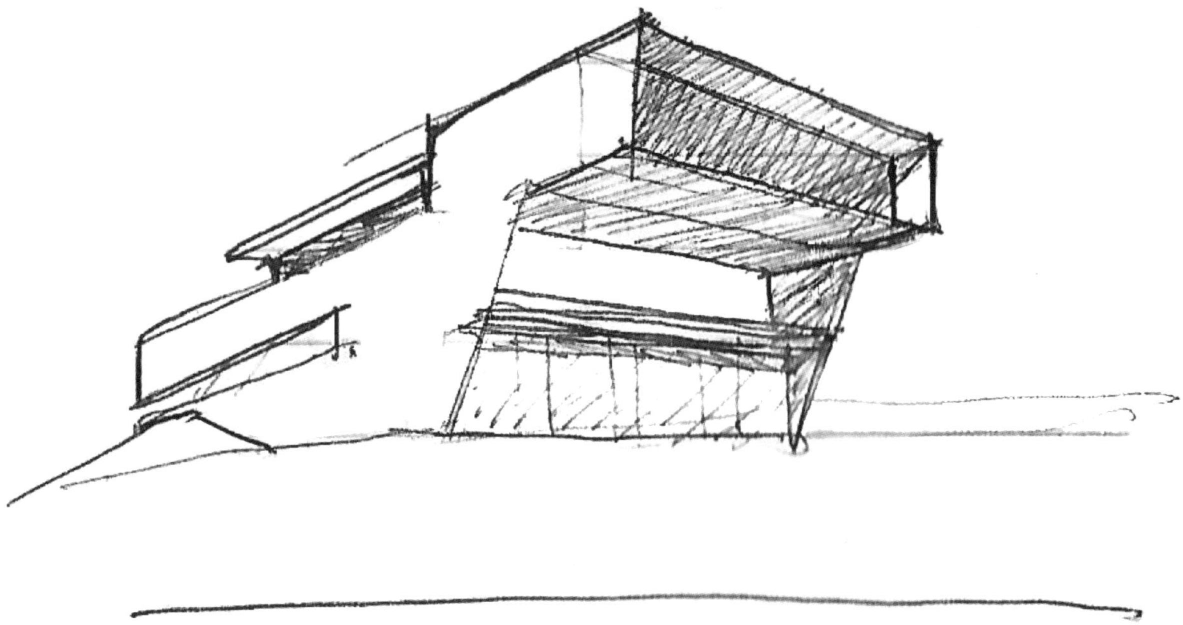

Early house version (above and right)

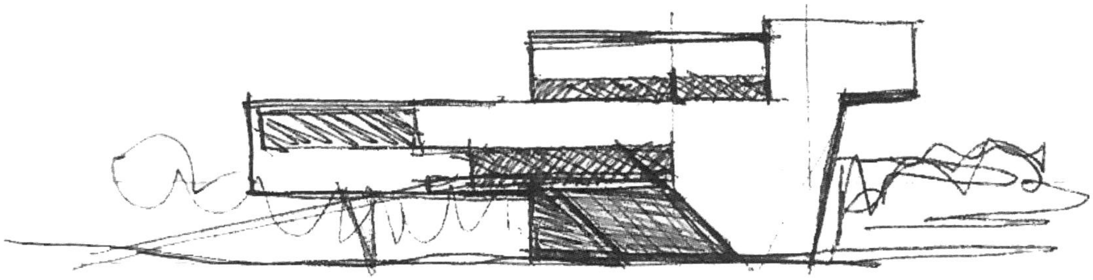

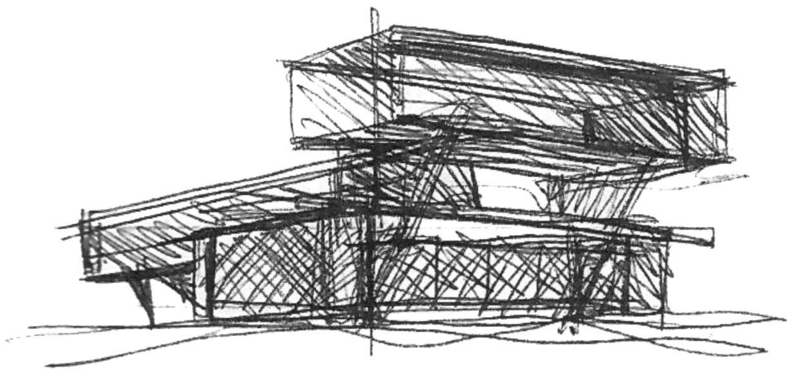

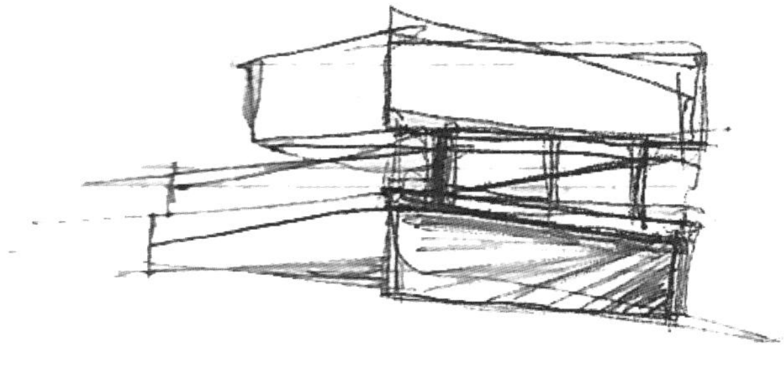

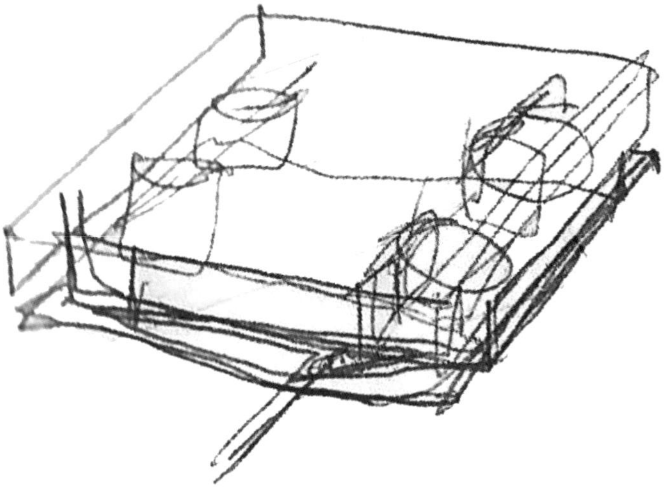

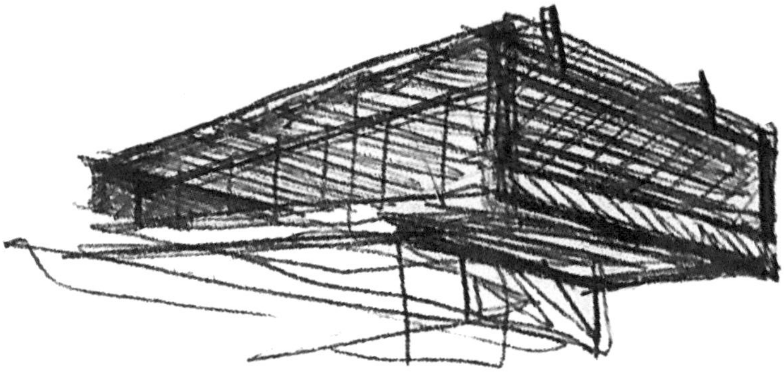

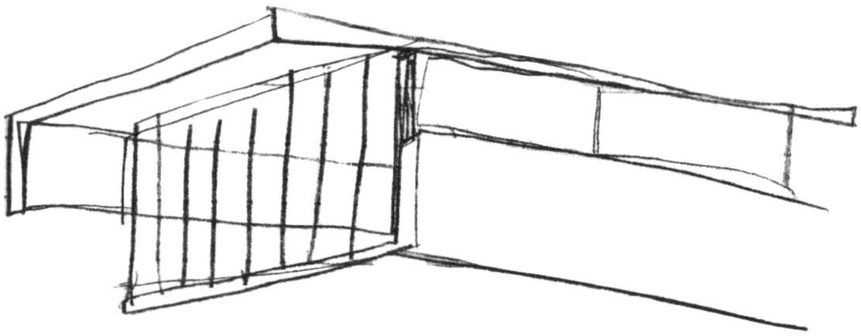

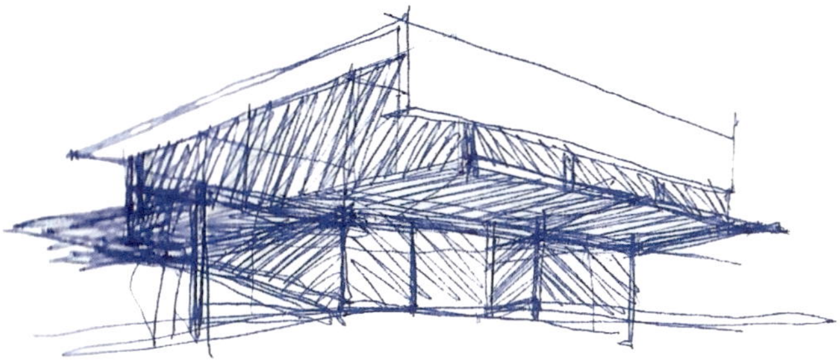

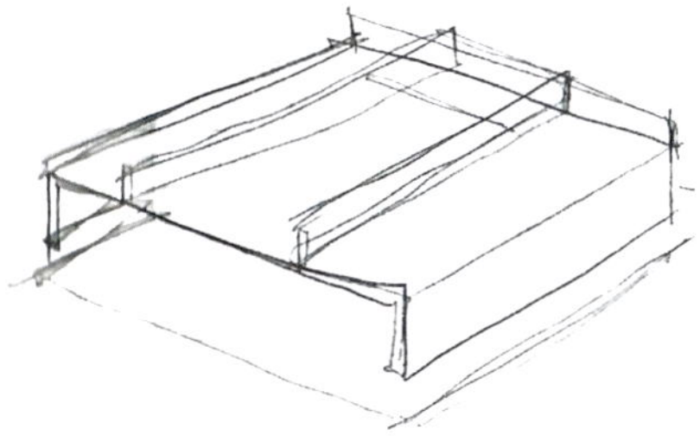

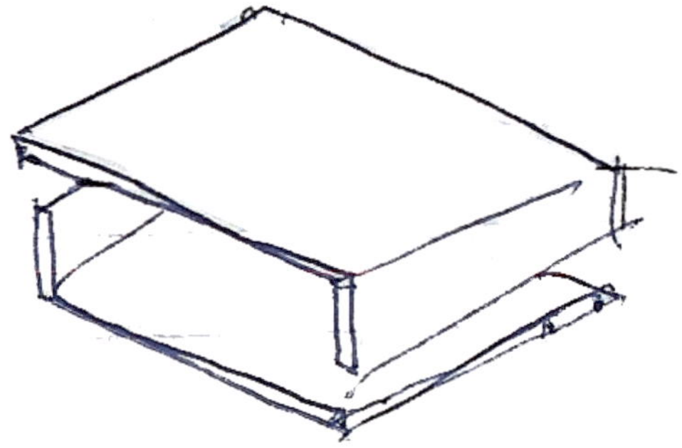

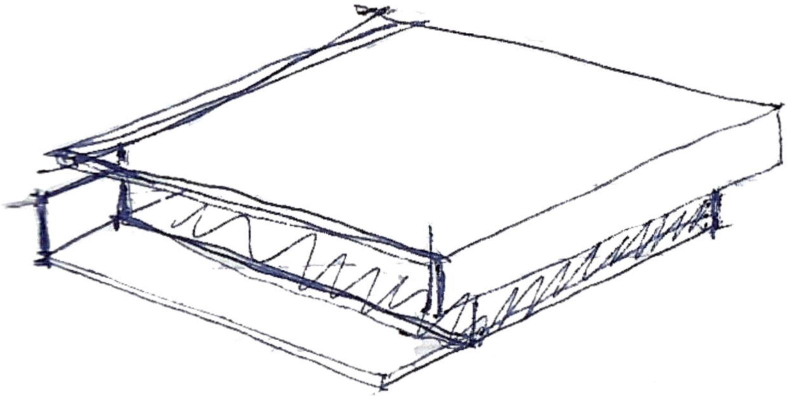

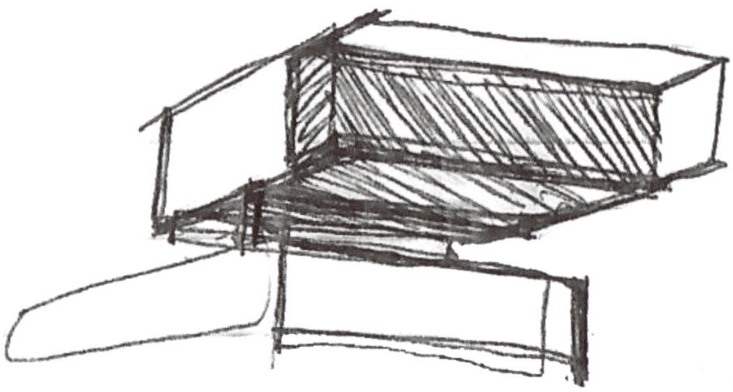

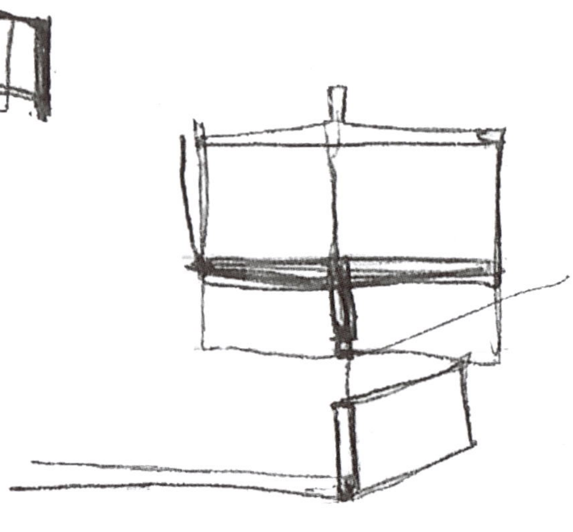

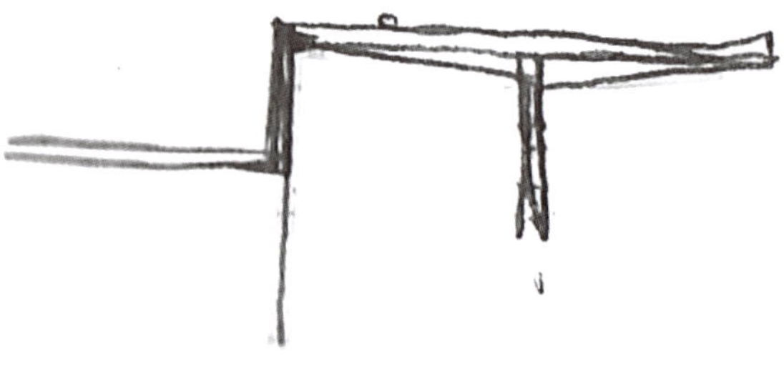

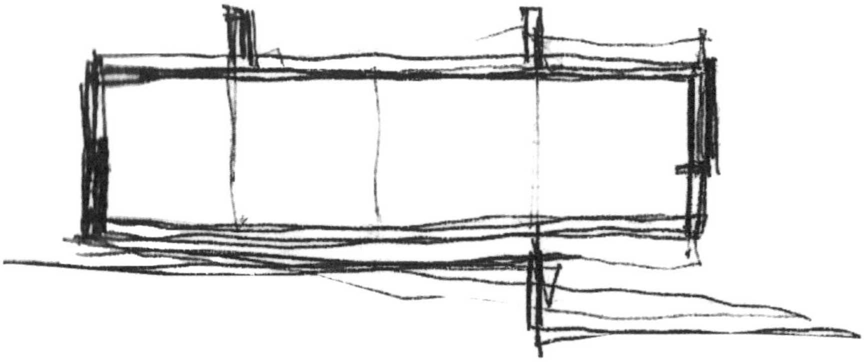

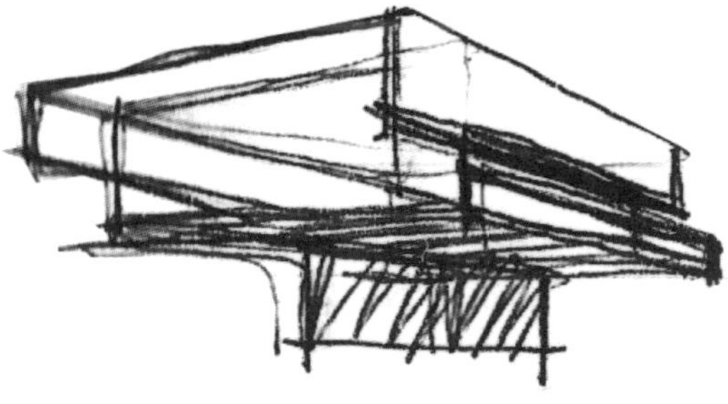

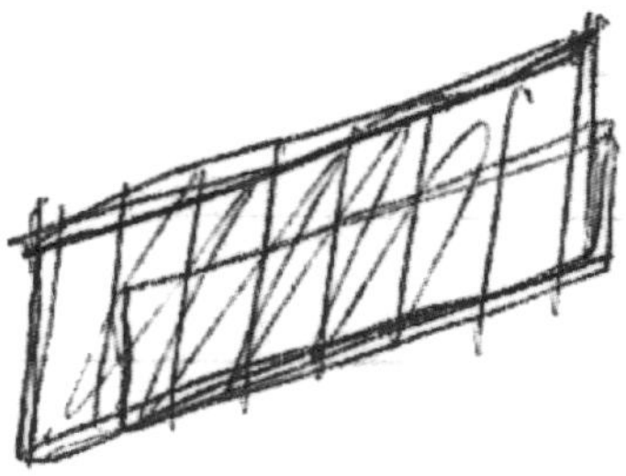

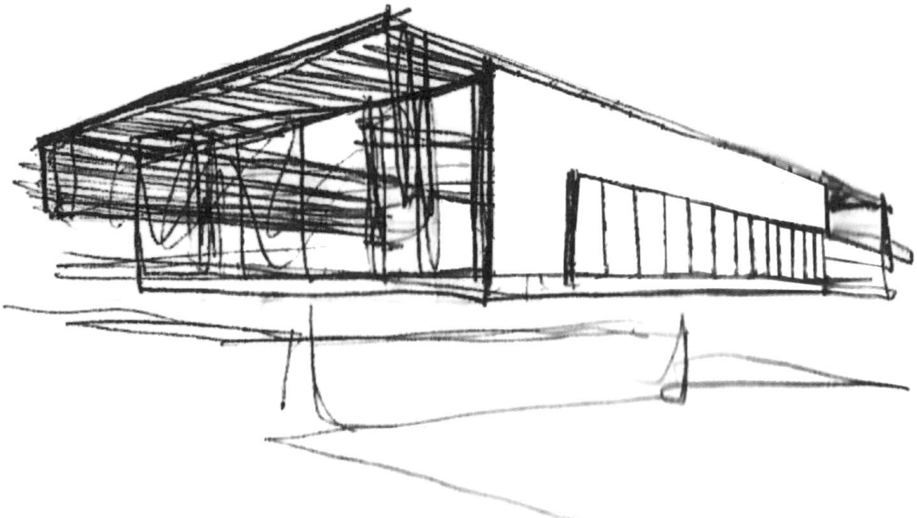

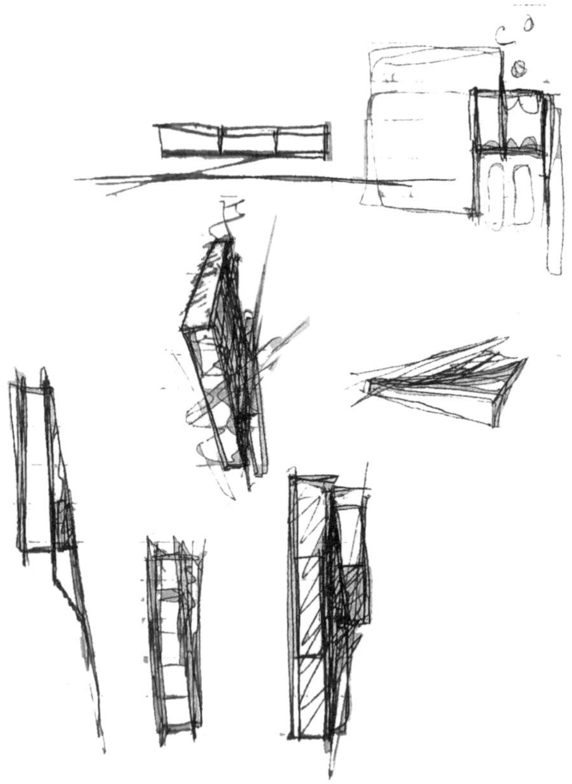

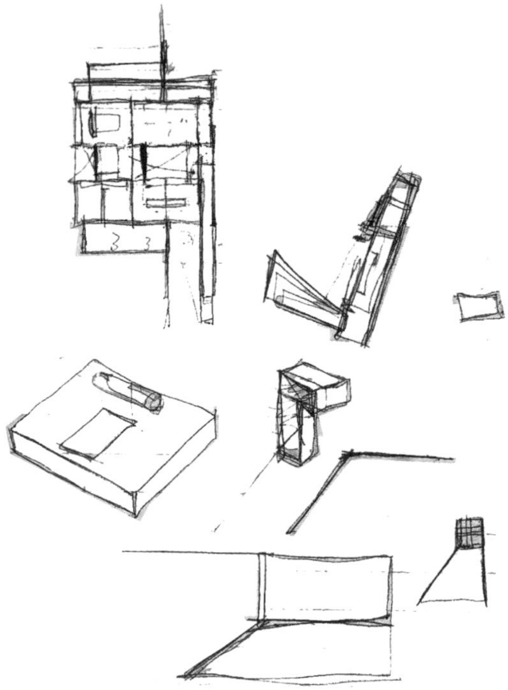

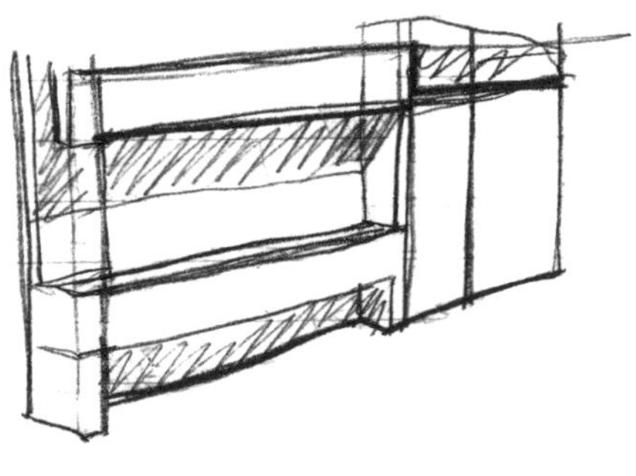

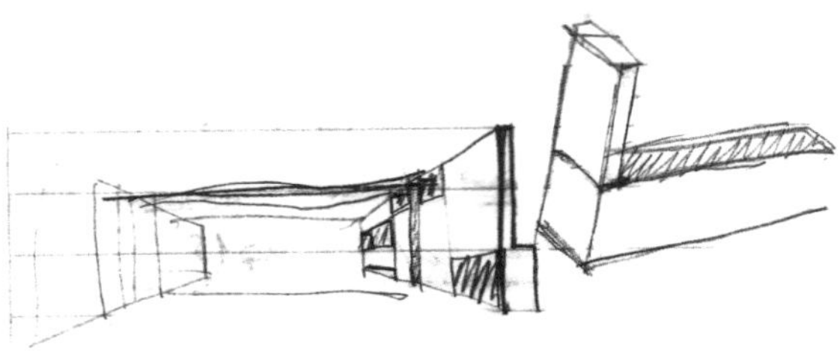

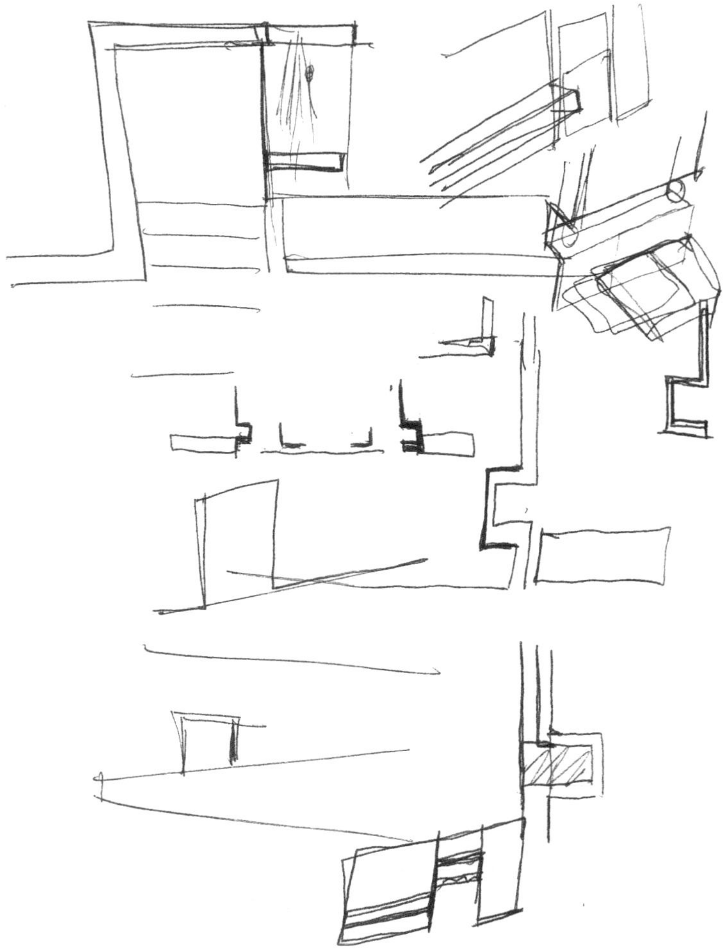

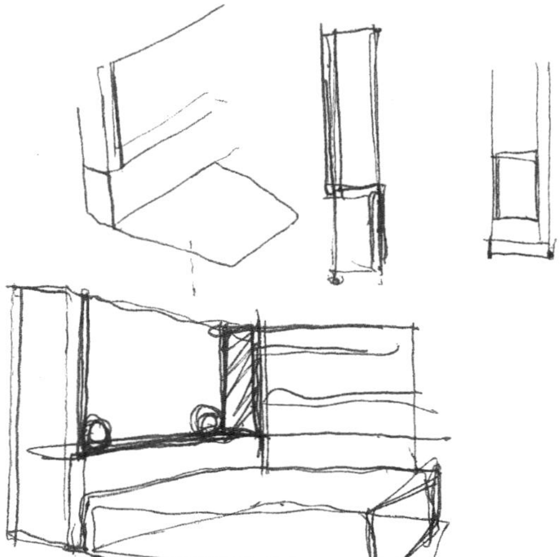

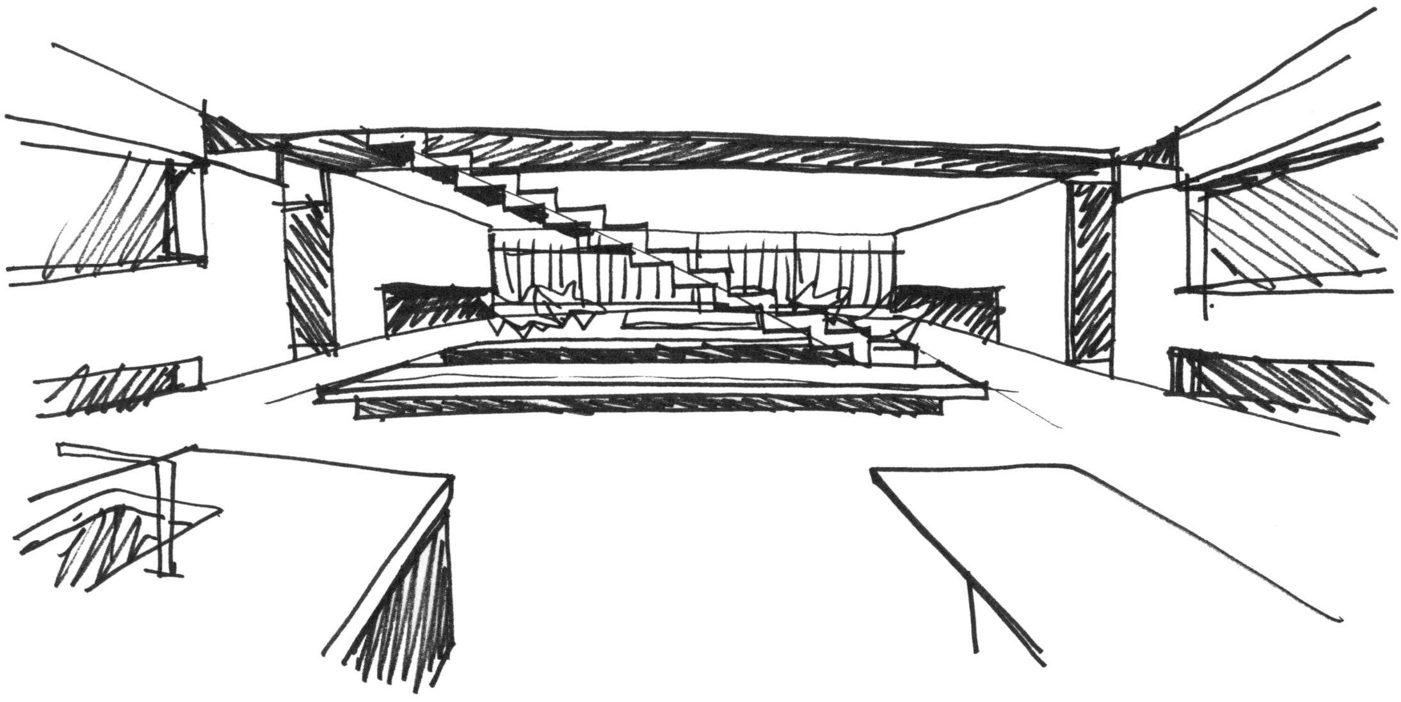

PRESENTATION DRAWINGS

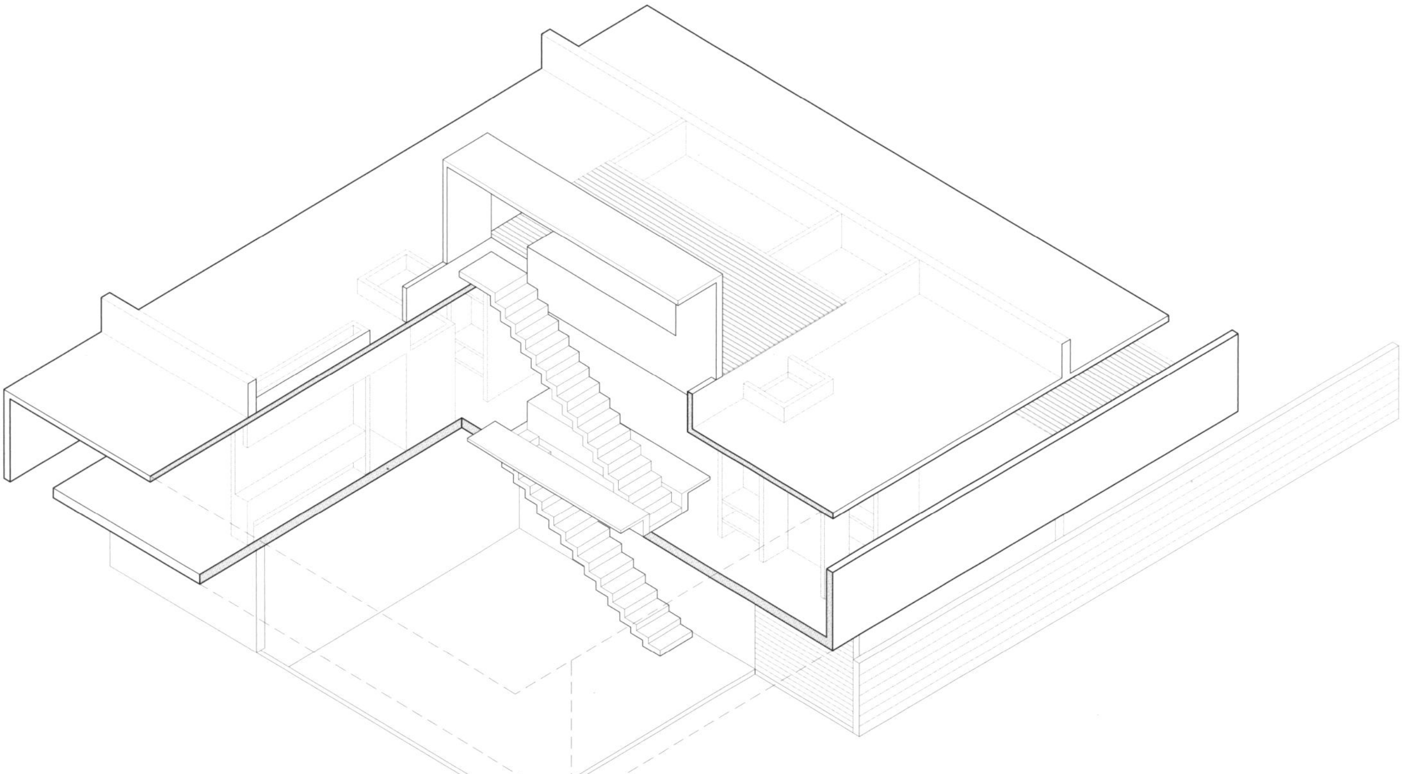

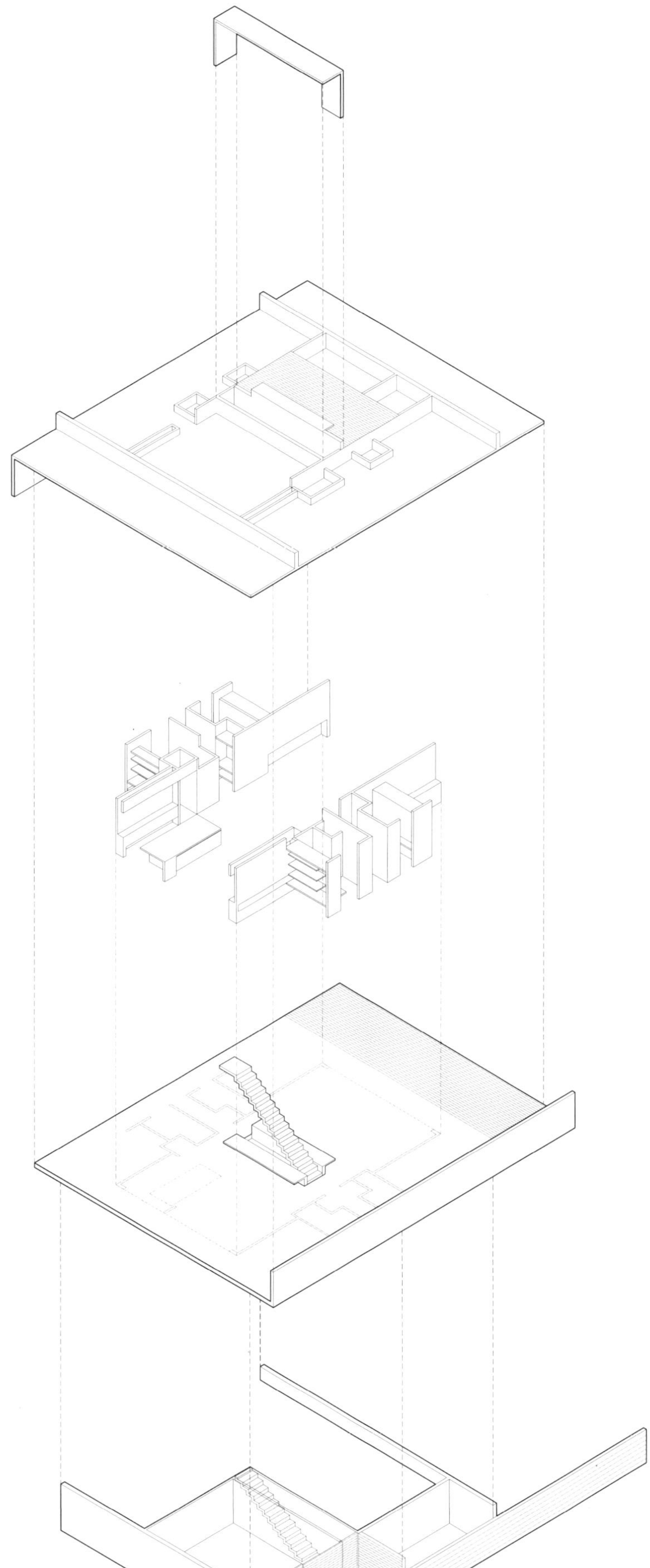

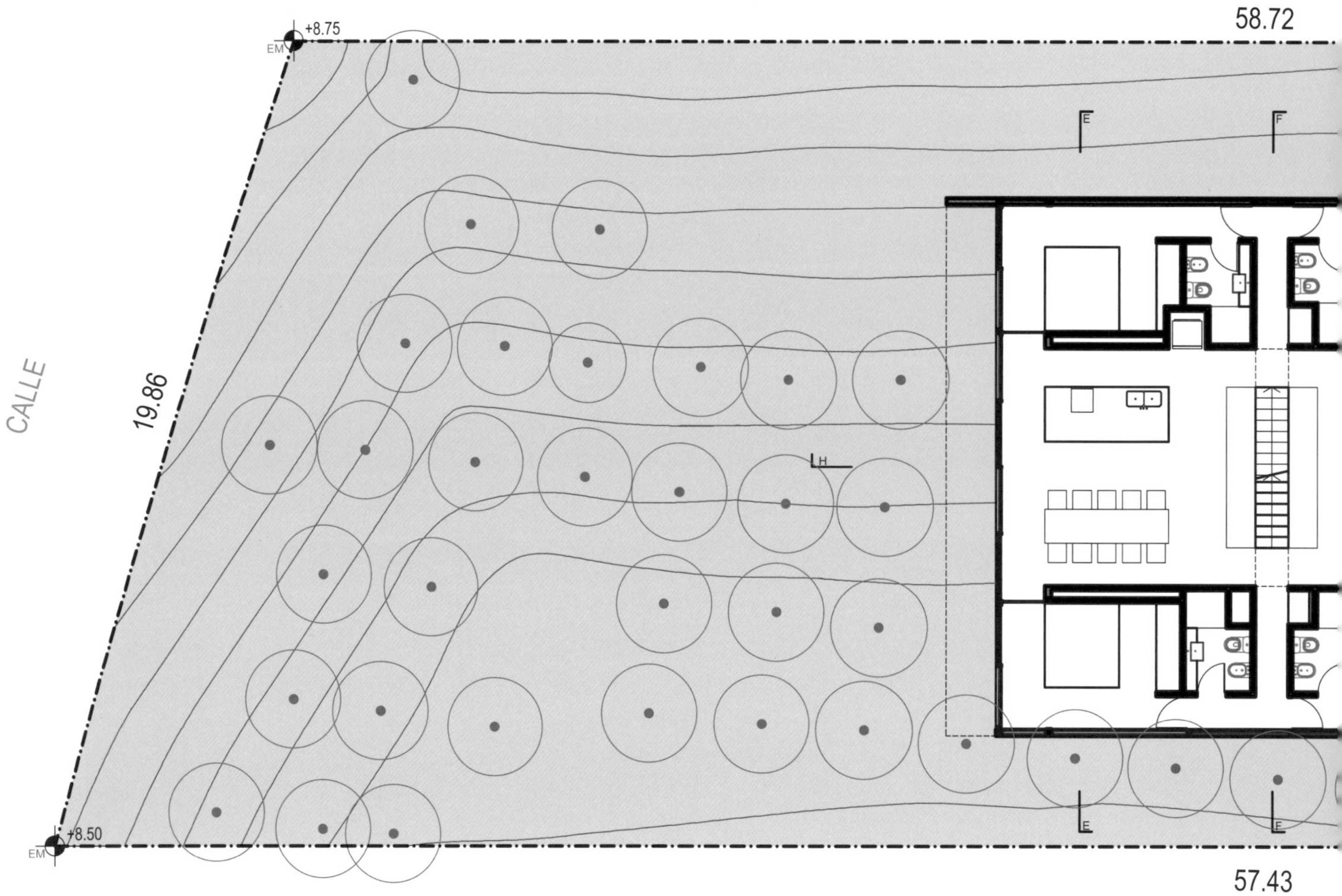

CASA L4 - PLANTA GENERAL

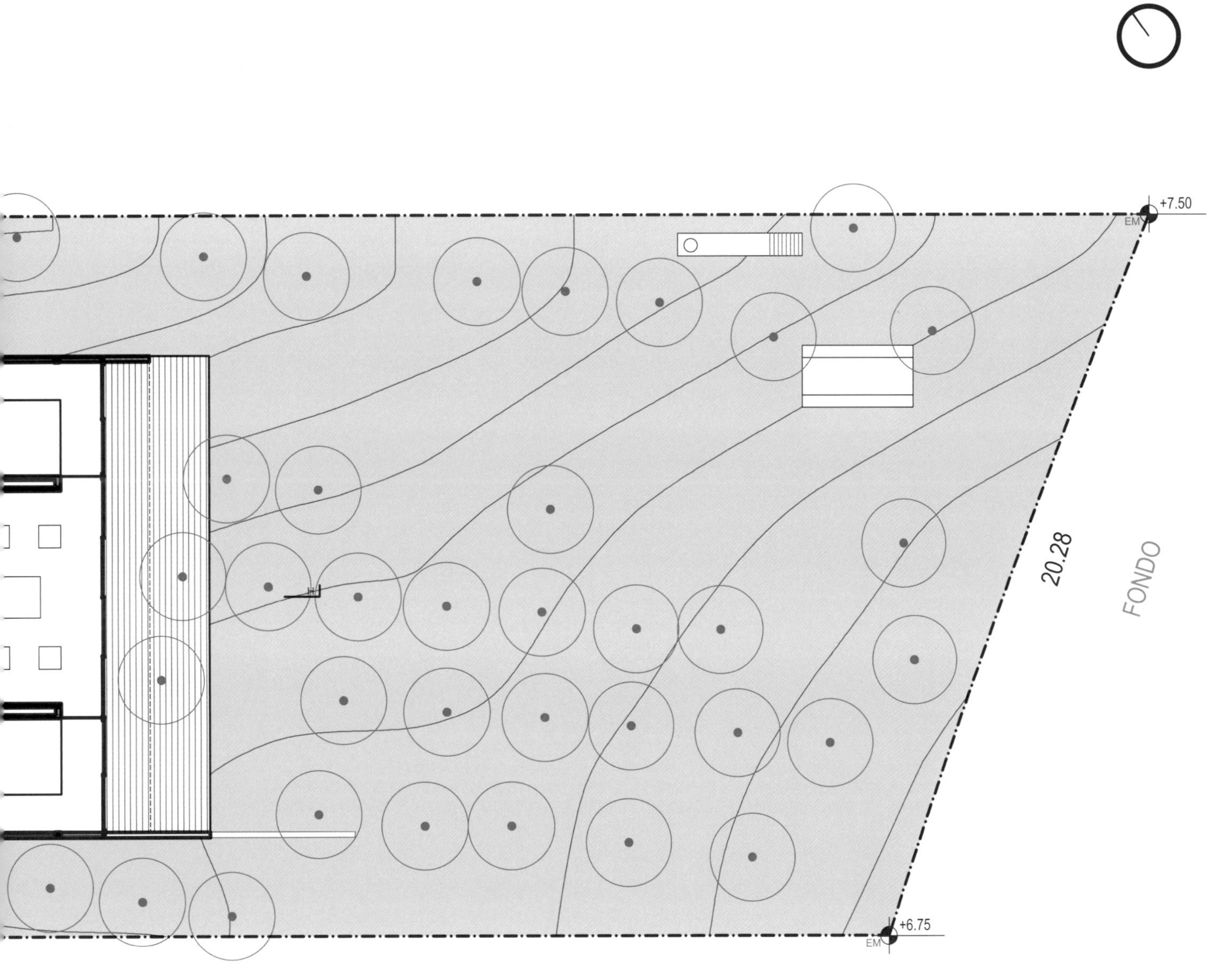
+7.50
EM
20.28
FONDO
+6.75
EM

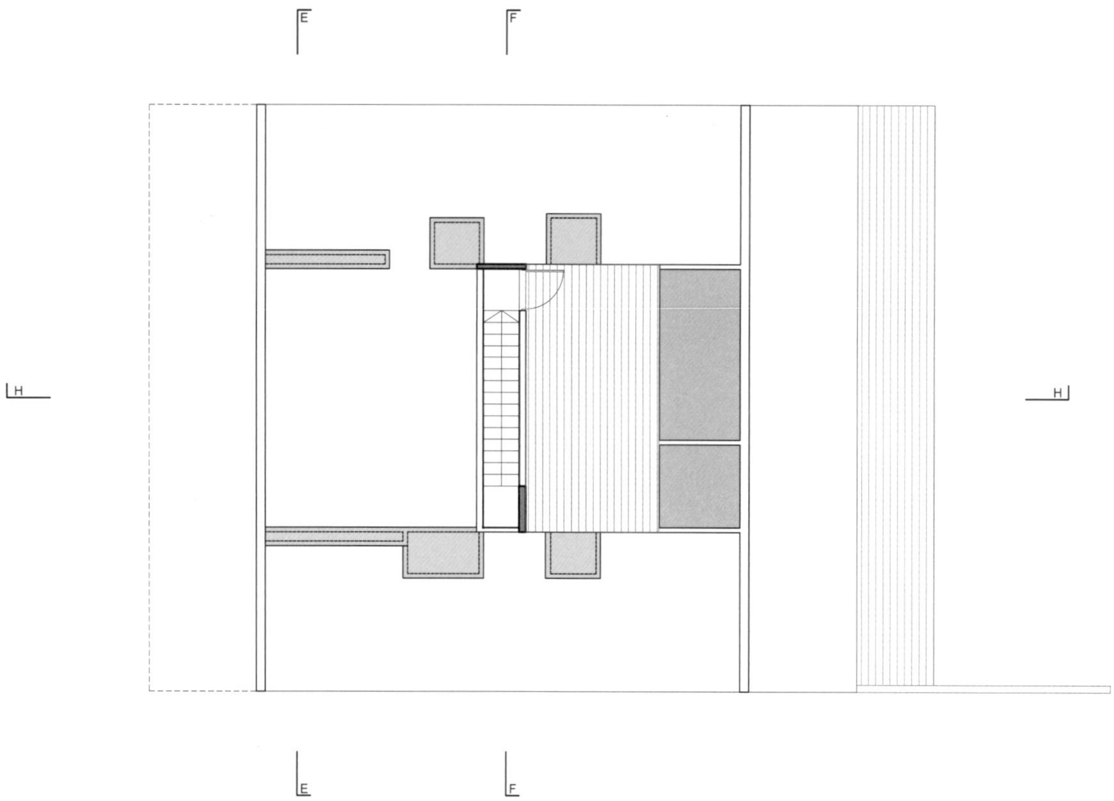

CASA L4 - PLANTA ALTA

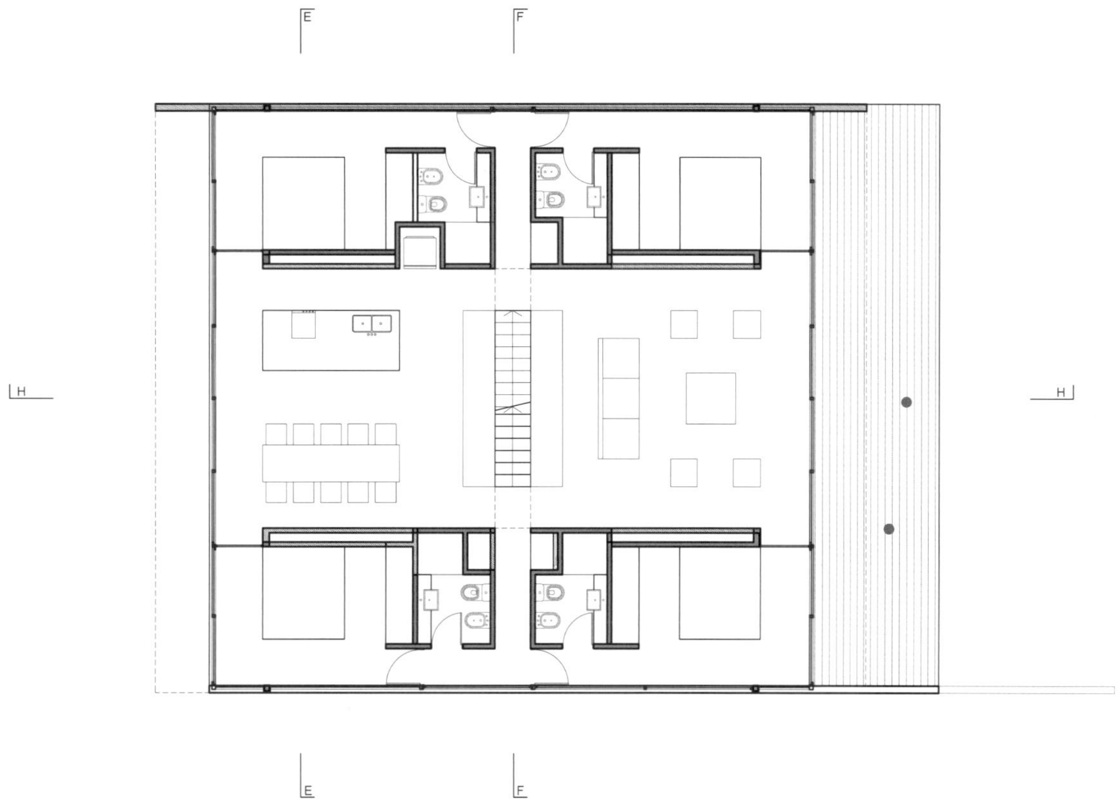

CASA L4 - PLANTA PRINCIPAL

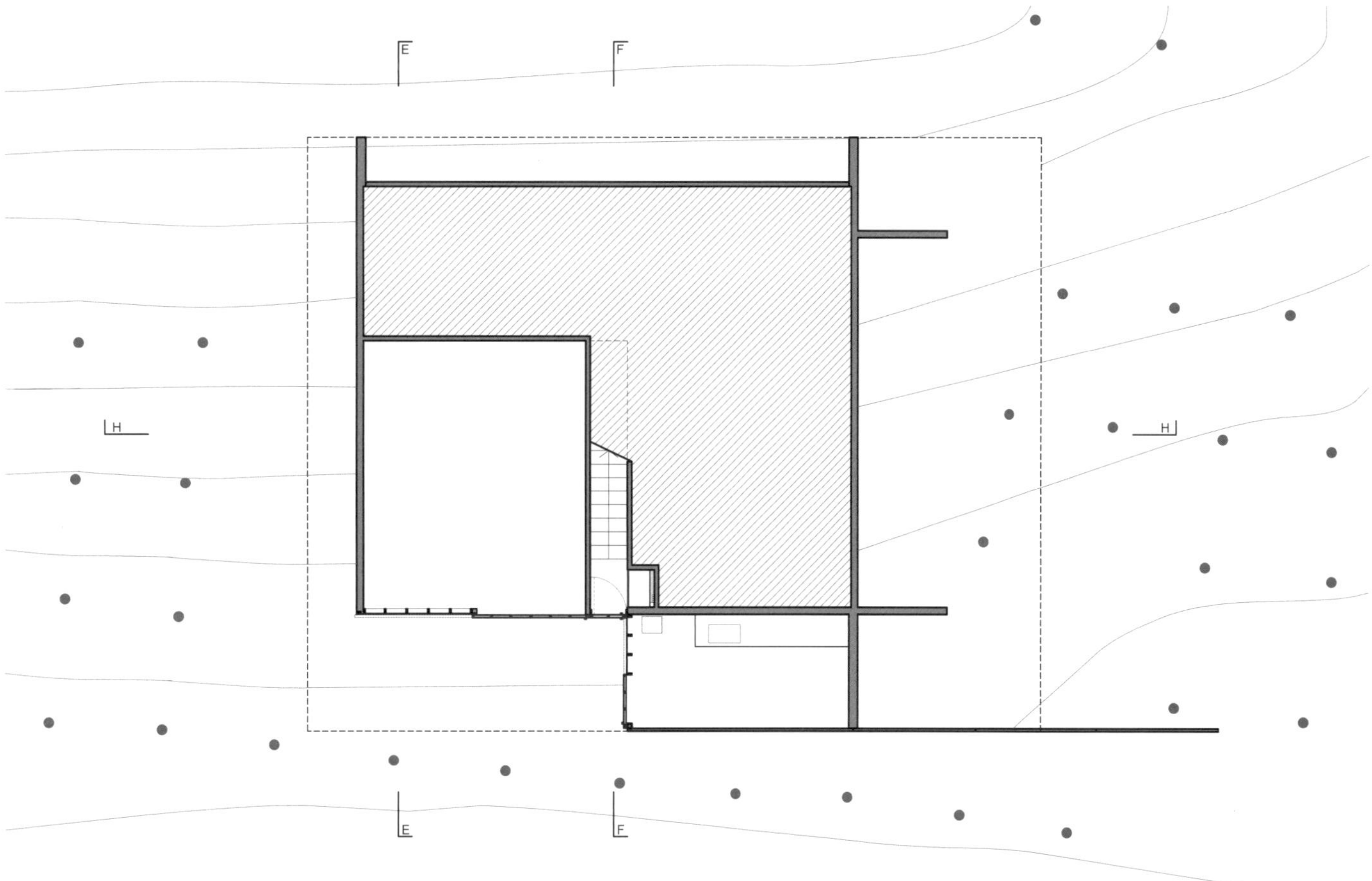

CASA L4 - PLANTA BAJA

1 5 10

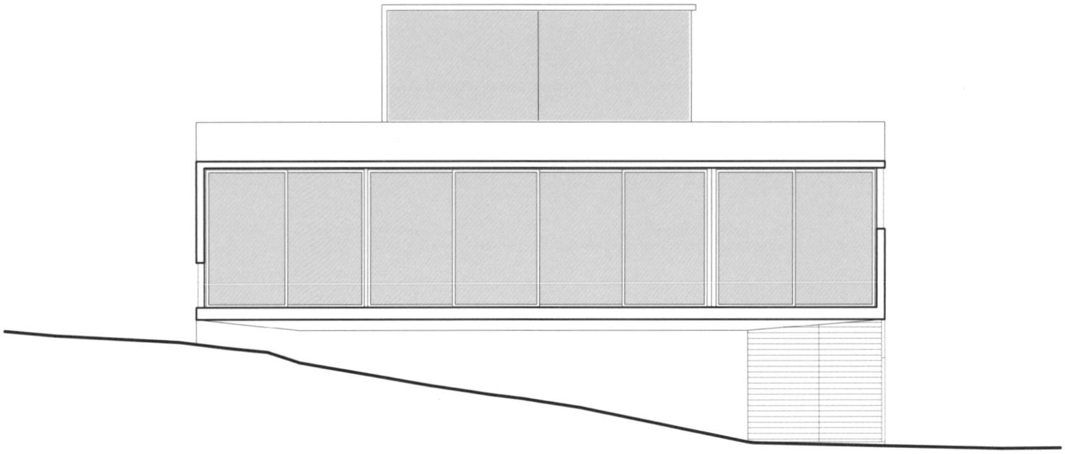

CASA L4 - VISTA FRENTE

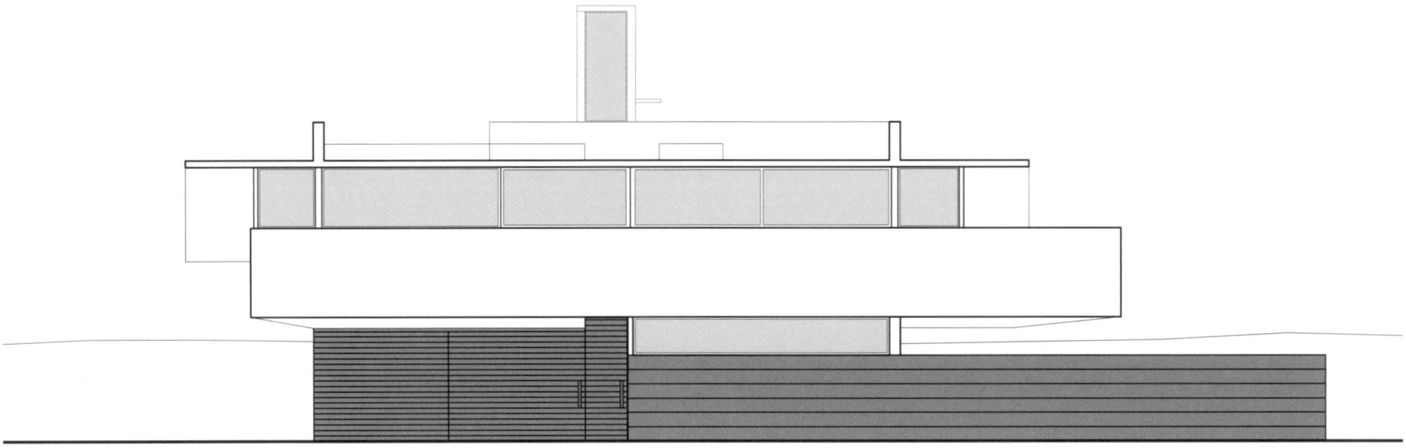

CASA L4 - VISTA LATERAL DERECHO

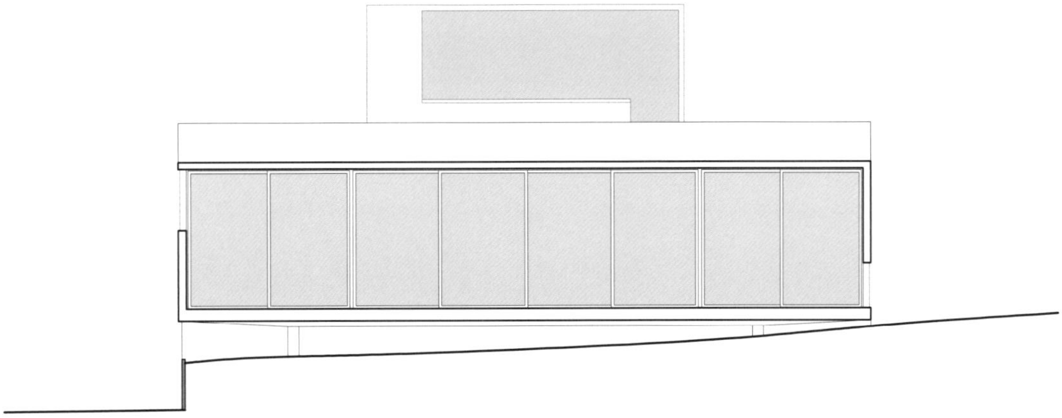

CASA L4 - VISTA CONTRAFRENTE

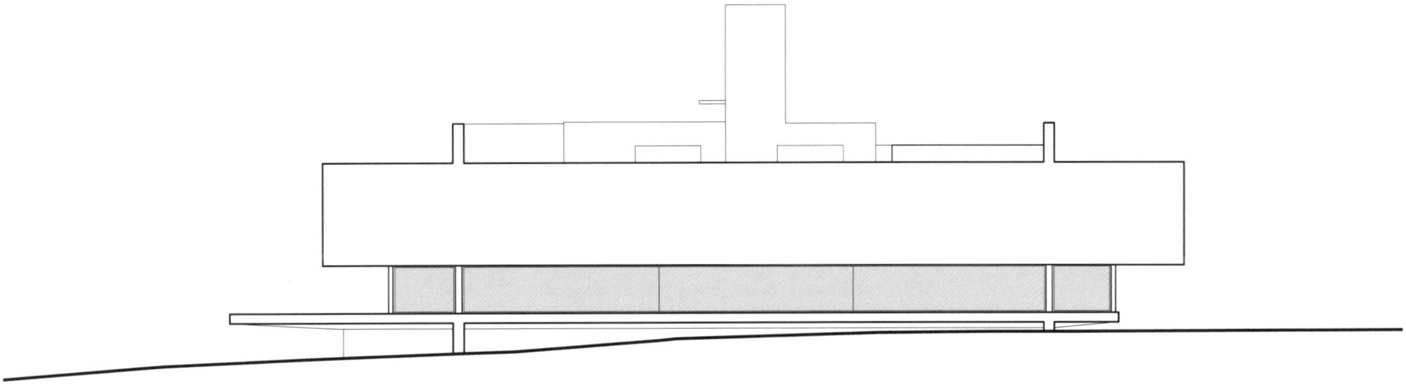

CASA L4 - VISTA LATERAL IZQUIERDO

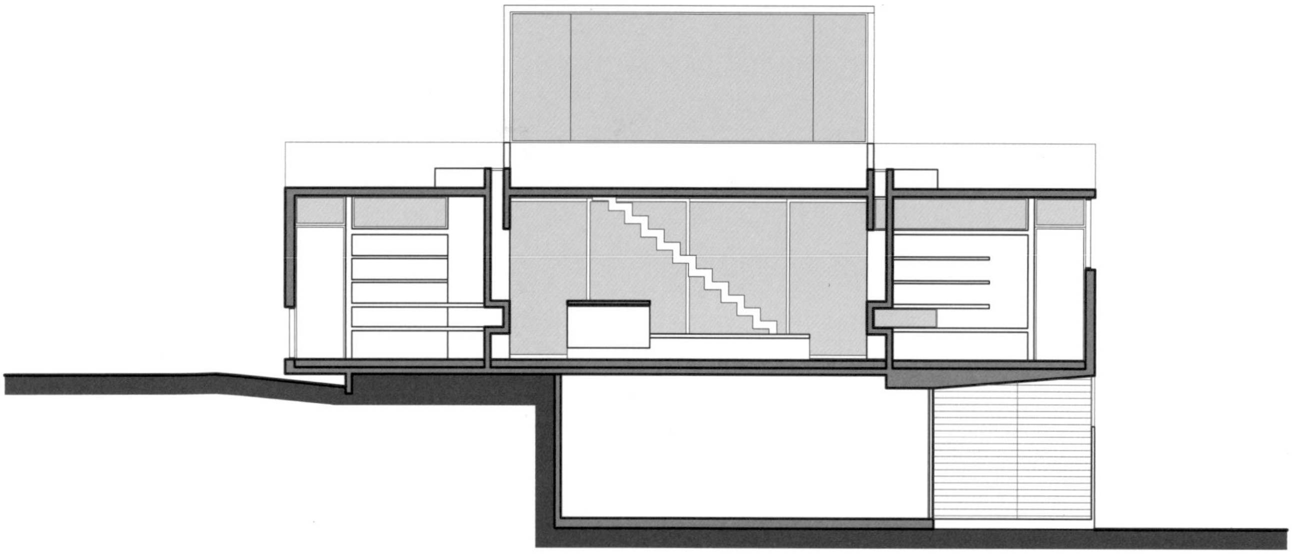

CASA L4 - CORTE E:E

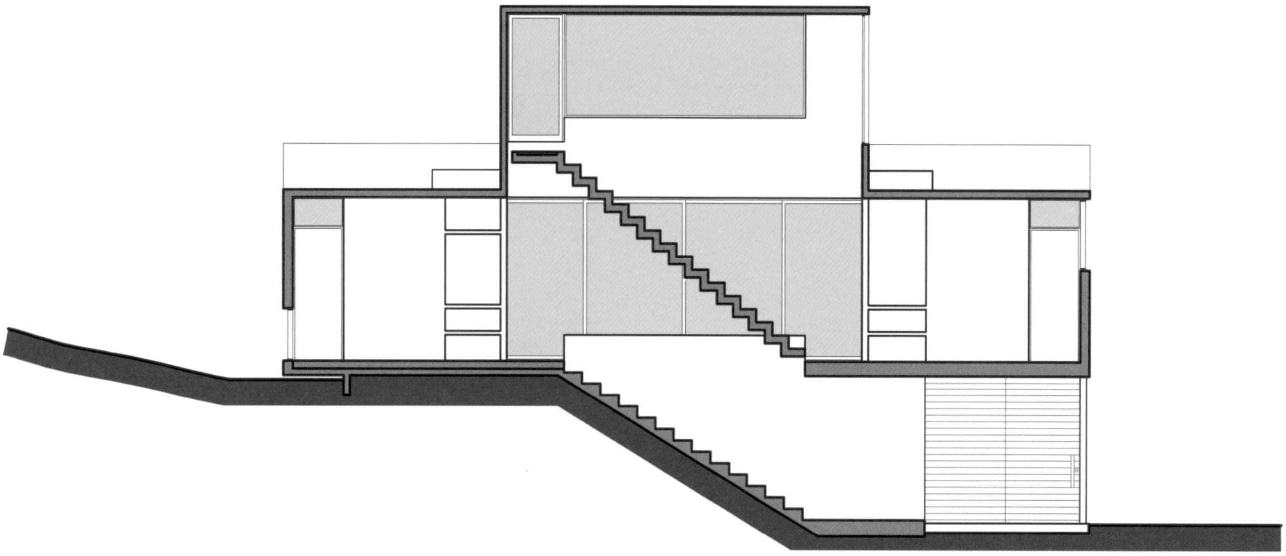

CASA L4 - CORTE F:F

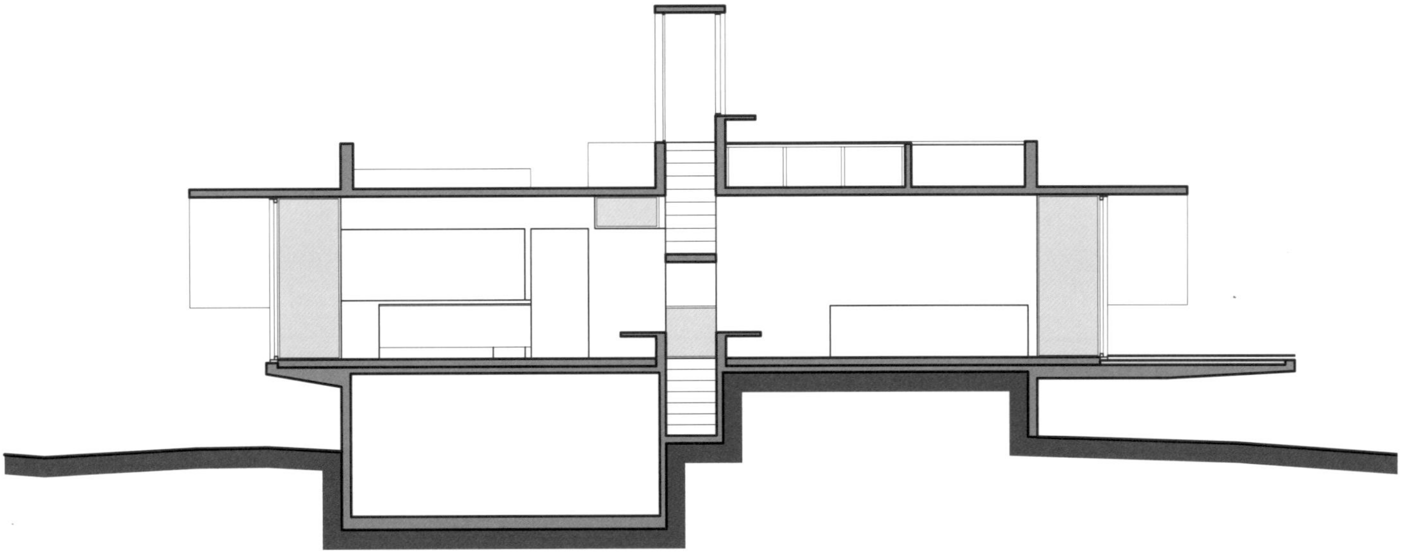

CASA L4 - CORTE H:H

CONSTRUCTION

WORKING DRAWINGS

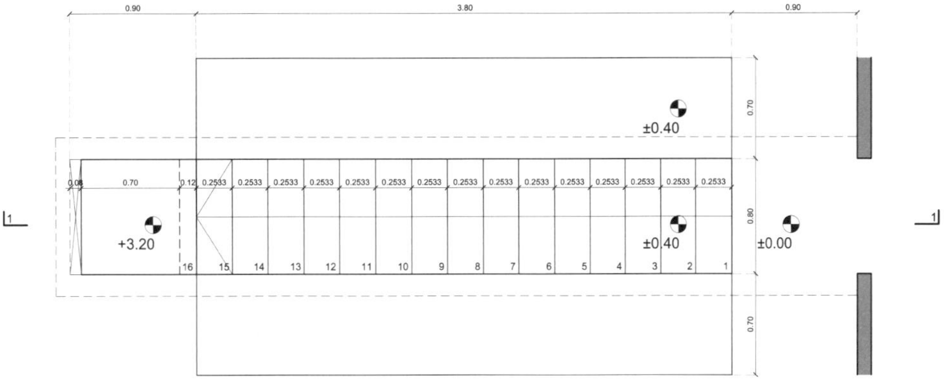
0.90
3.80
0.90
±0.40
+3.20
±0.40
±0.00
0.70
0.80
0.70

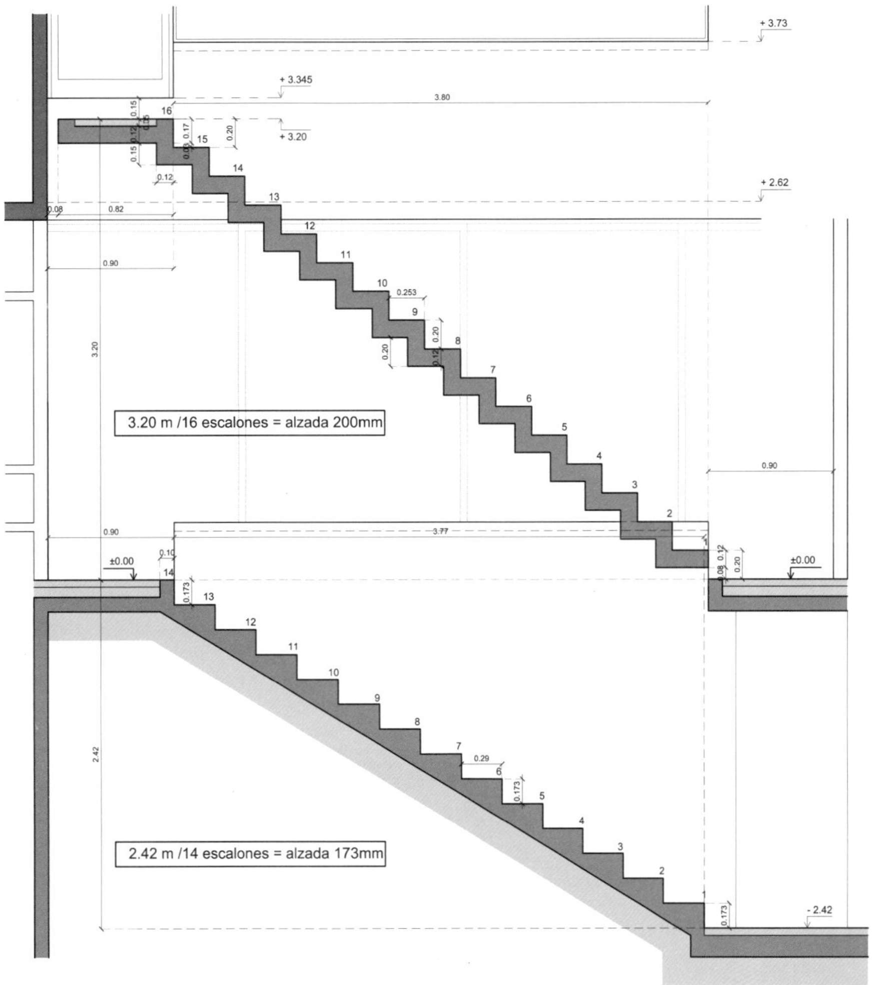
+ 3.73
+ 3.345
3.80
+ 3.20
+ 2.62
3.20 m /16 escalones = alzada 200mm
±0.00
±0.00
2.42 m /14 escalones = alzada 173mm
- 2.42

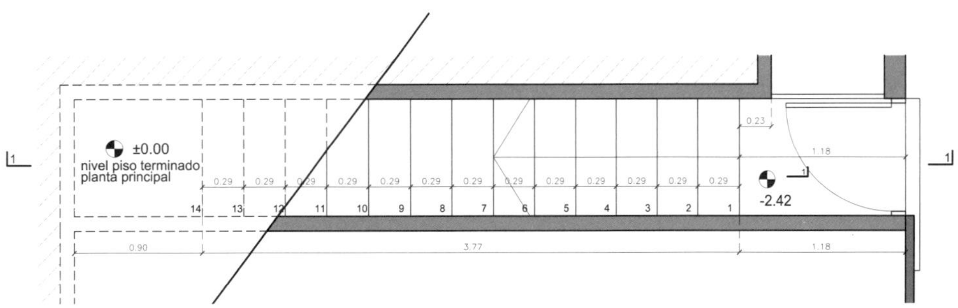
±0.00
nivel piso terminado
planta principal
-2.42
0.90
3.77
1.18

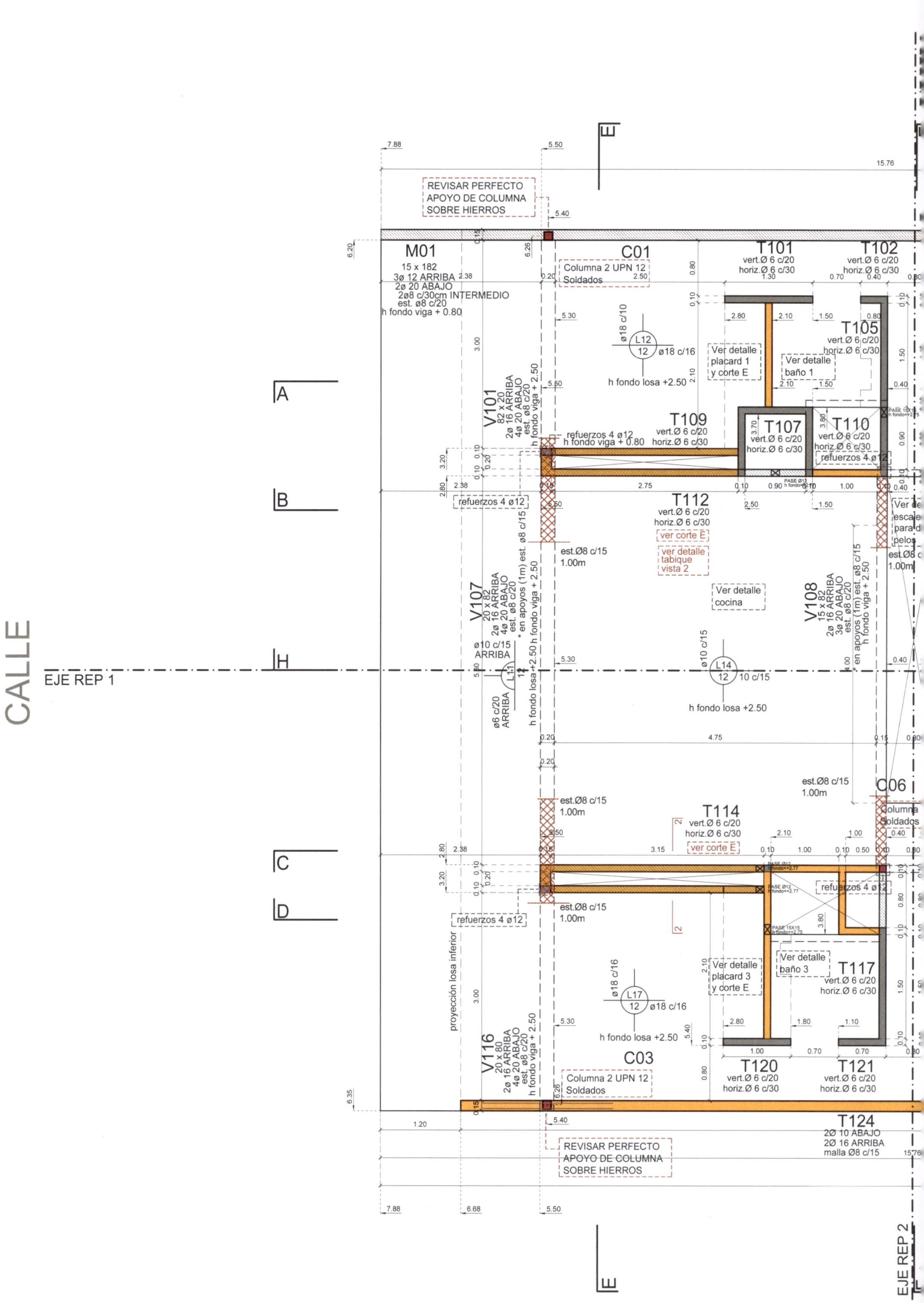
CALLE
EJE REP 1
EJE REP 2
REVISAR PERFECTO APOYO DE COLUMNA SOBRE HIERROS
M01
15 x 182
3ø 12 ARRIBA
2ø 20 ABAJO
2ø8 c/30cm INTERMEDIO
est. ø8 c/20
h fondo viga + 0.80
C01
Columna 2 UPN 12 Soldados
T101
vert.Ø 6 c/20
horiz.Ø 6 c/30
T102
vert.Ø 6 c/20
horiz.Ø 6 c/30
T105
vert.Ø 6 c/20
horiz.Ø 6 c/30
Ver detalle placard 1 y corte E
Ver detalle baño 1
h fondo losa +2.50
V101
82 x 20
2ø 16 ARRIBA
4ø 20 ABAJO
est. ø8 c/20
h fondo viga + 2.50
refuerzos 4 ø12
h fondo viga + 0.80
T109
vert.Ø 6 c/20
horiz.Ø 6 c/30
T107
vert.Ø 6 c/20
horiz.Ø 6 c/30
T110
vert.Ø 6 c/20
horiz.Ø 6 c/30
refuerzos 4 ø12
T112
vert.Ø 6 c/20
horiz.Ø 6 c/30
ver corte E
ver detalle tabique vista 2
Ver detalle cocina
est.Ø8 c/15
1.00m
V107
20 x 82
2ø 16 ARRIBA
4ø 20 ABAJO
est. ø8 c/20
* en apoyos (1m) est. ø8 c/15
h fondo viga + 2.50
V108
15 x 82
2ø 16 ARRIBA
3ø 20 ABAJO
est. ø8 c/20
* en apoyos (1m) est. ø8 c/15
h fondo viga + 2.50
ø10 c/15 ARRIBA
ø6 c/20 ARRIBA
h fondo losa +2.50
C06
Columna Soldados
T114
vert.Ø 6 c/20
horiz.Ø 6 c/30
ver corte E
refuerzos 4 ø12
Ver detalle placard 3 y corte E
Ver detalle baño 3
T117
vert.Ø 6 c/20
horiz.Ø 6 c/30
proyección losa inferior
V116
20 x 80
2ø 16 ARRIBA
4ø 20 ABAJO
est. ø8 c/20
h fondo viga + 2.50
C03
Columna 2 UPN 12 Soldados
T120
vert.Ø 6 c/20
horiz.Ø 6 c/30
T121
vert.Ø 6 c/20
horiz.Ø 6 c/30
T124
2Ø 10 ABAJO
2Ø 16 ARRIBA
malla Ø8 c/15

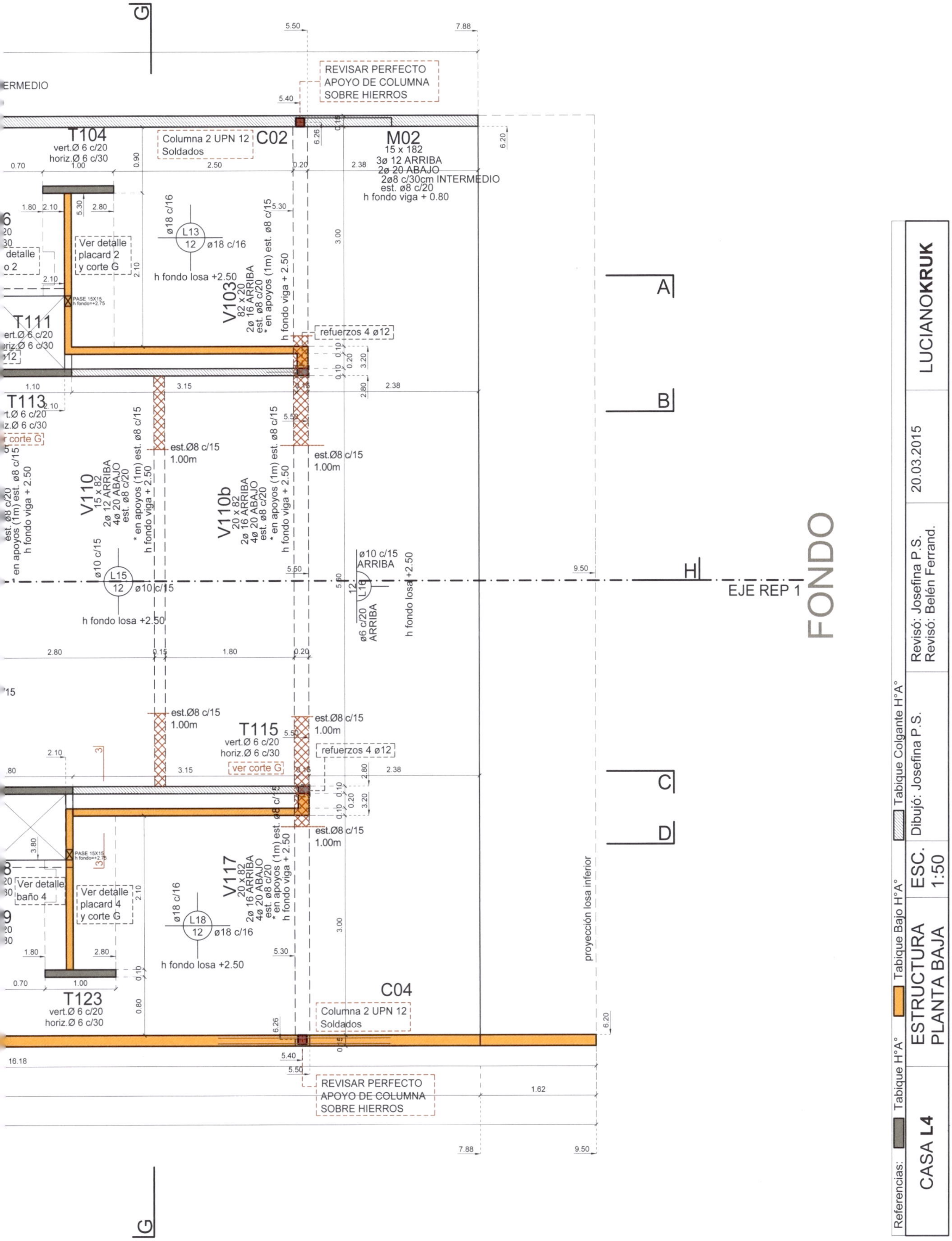
FONDO
EJE REP 1
Referencias: Tabique H°A° Tabique Bajo H°A° Tabique Colgante H°A°
CASA L4
ESTRUCTURA PLANTA BAJA
ESC. 1:50
Dibujó: Josefina P.S.
Revisó: Josefina P.S.
Revisó: Belén Ferrand.
20.03.2015
LUCIANOKRUK

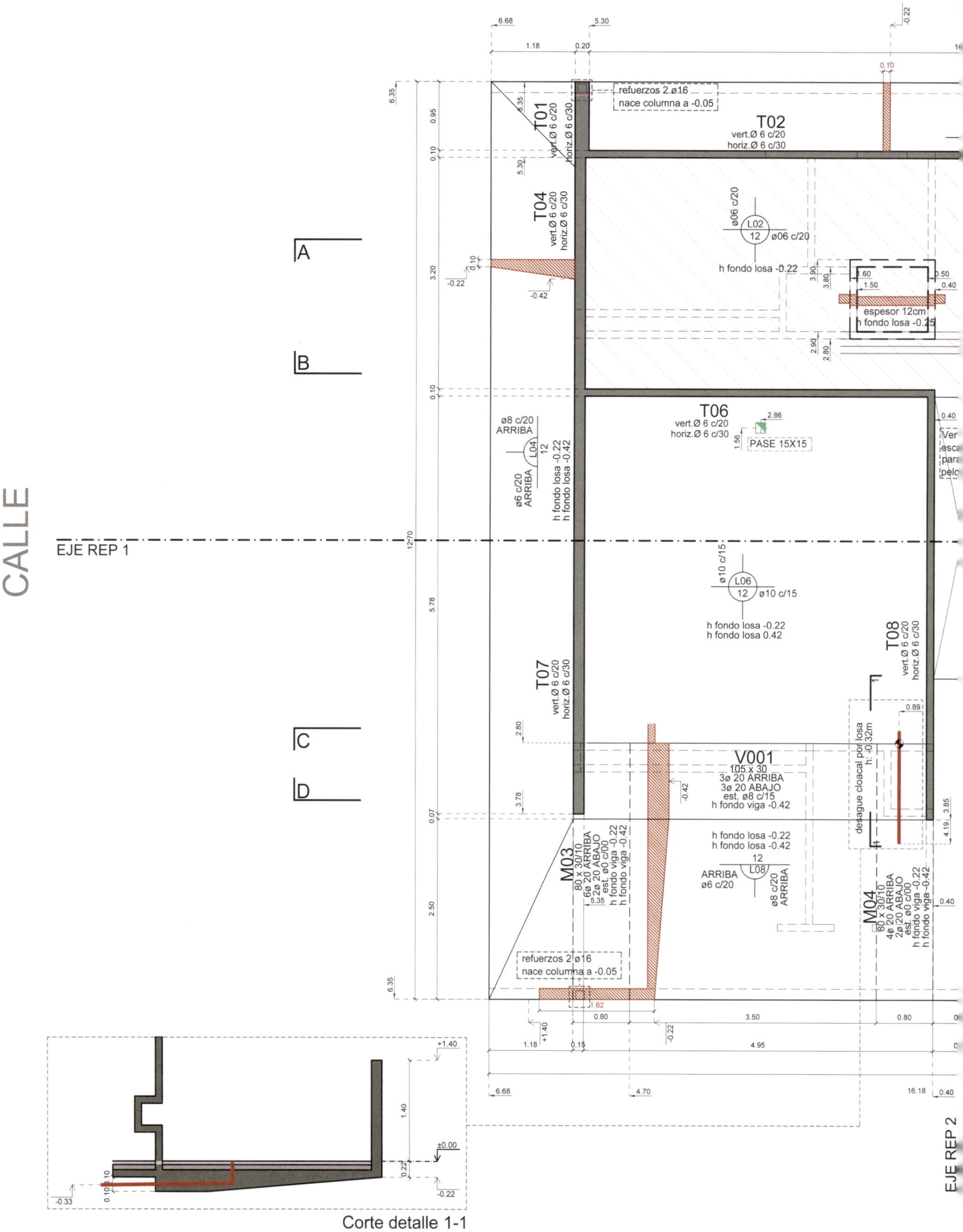

Corte detalle 1-1

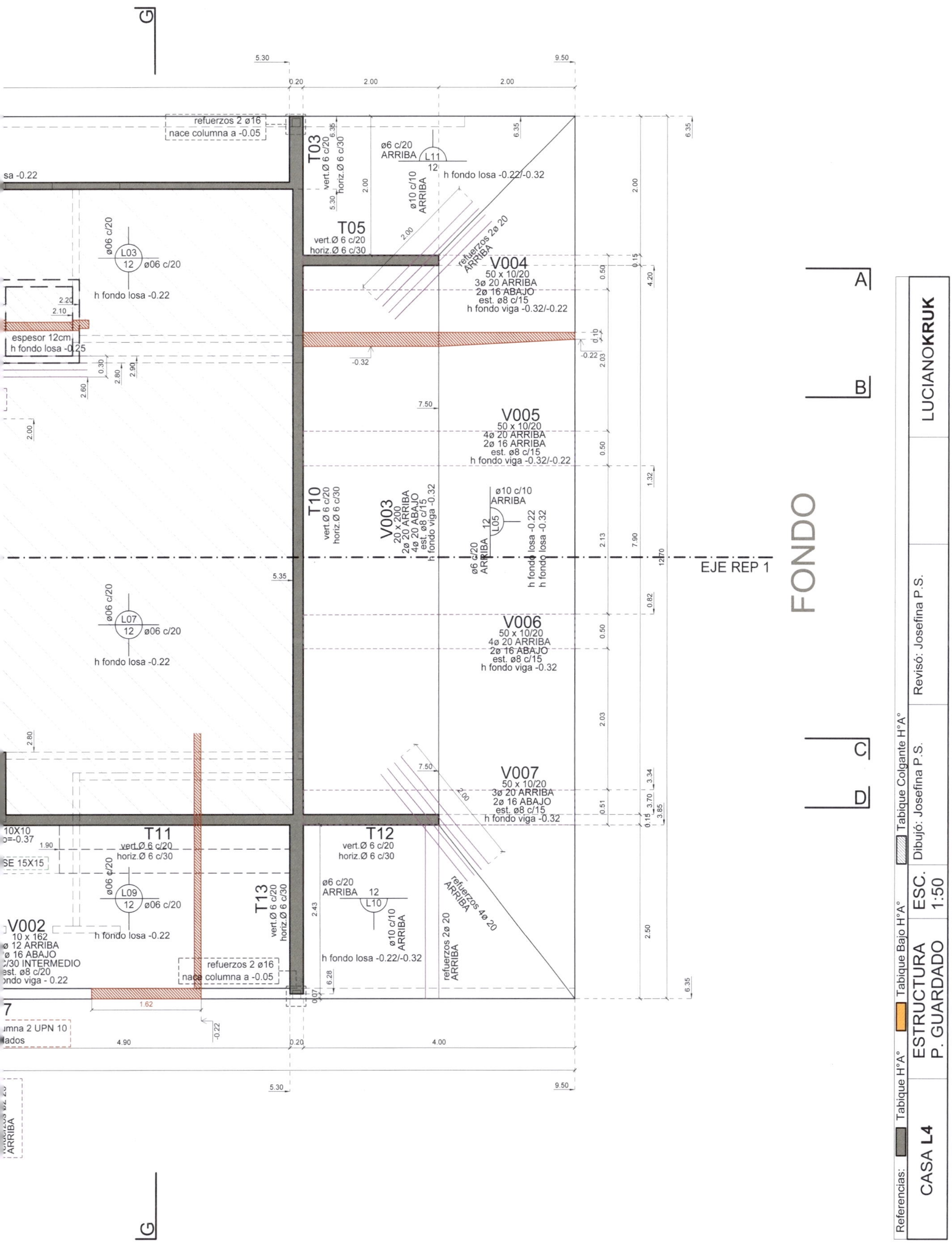

CASA L4
ESTRUCTURA
P. GUARDADO
ESC. 1:50
Dibujó: Josefina P.S.
Revisó: Josefina P.S.
LUCIANOKRUK
Referencias:
Tabique H°A°
Tabique Bajo H°A°
Tabique Colgante H°A°
FONDO
EJE REP 1
V004
50 x 10/20
3ø 20 ARRIBA
2ø 16 ABAJO
est. ø8 c/15
h fondo viga -0.32/-0.22
V005
50 x 10/20
4ø 20 ARRIBA
2ø 16 ARRIBA
est. ø8 c/15
h fondo viga -0.32/-0.22
V006
50 x 10/20
4ø 20 ARRIBA
2ø 16 ABAJO
est. ø8 c/15
h fondo viga -0.32
V007
50 x 10/20
3ø 20 ARRIBA
2ø 16 ABAJO
est. ø8 c/15
h fondo viga -0.32
V003
20 x 200
2ø 20 ARRIBA
4ø 20 ABAJO
est. ø8 c/15
h fondo viga -0.32
T03
T05
T10
T11
T12
T13
vert.Ø 6 c/20
horiz.Ø 6 c/30
L03
L05
L07
L09
L10
L11
ø06 c/20
h fondo losa -0.22
h fondo losa -0.22/-0.32
ø10 c/10 ARRIBA
ø6 c/20 ARRIBA
refuerzos 2 ø16
nace columna a -0.05
refuerzos 2ø 20 ARRIBA
refuerzos 4ø 20 ARRIBA
espesor 12cm
h fondo losa -0.25
V002
10 x 162

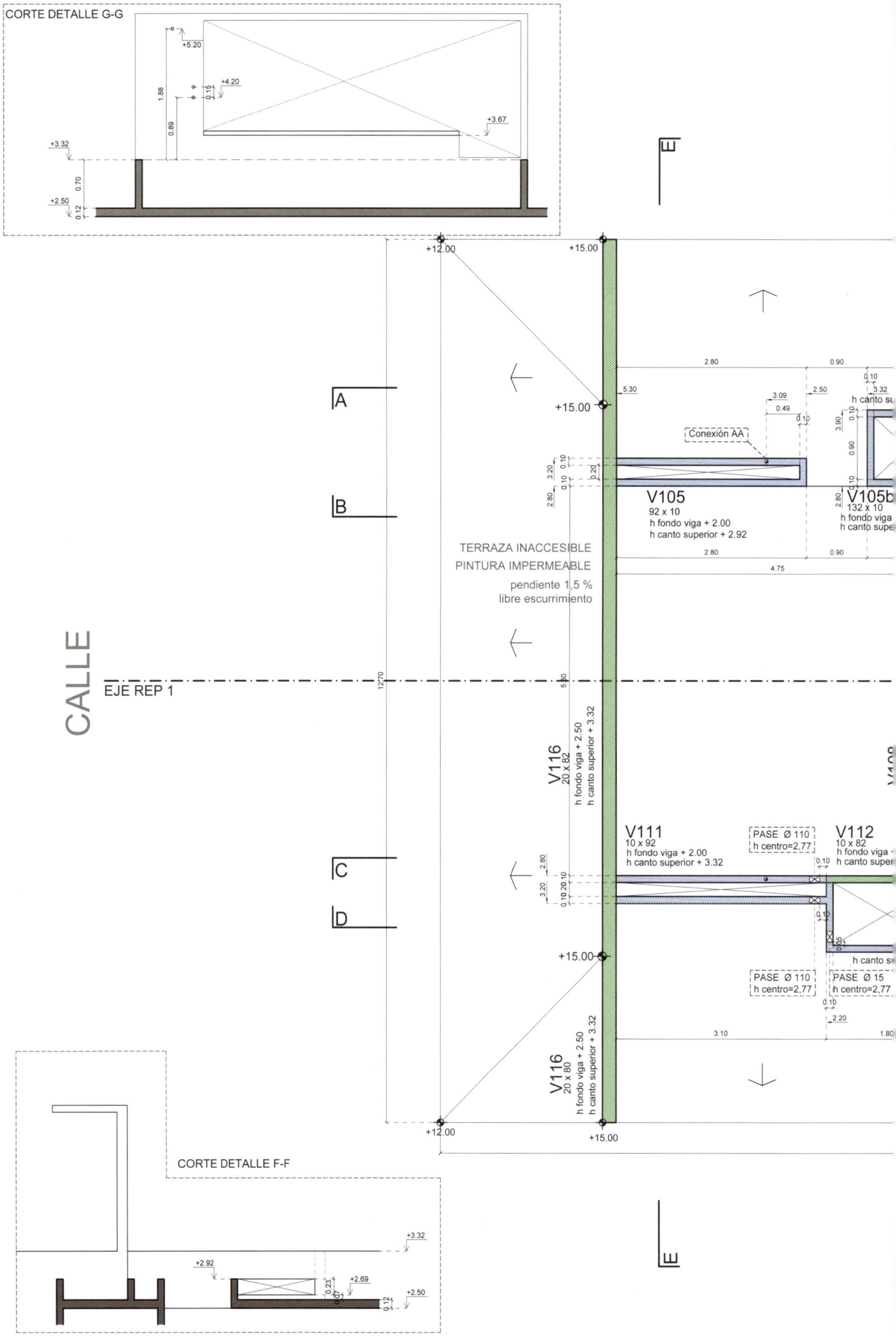
CORTE DETALLE G-G
+5.20
+4.20
+3.67
+3.32
+2.50
1.88
0.89
0.15
0.70
0.12
CALLE
EJE REP 1
A
B
C
D
E
+12.00
+15.00
TERRAZA INACCESIBLE
PINTURA IMPERMEABLE
pendiente 1,5 %
libre escurrimiento
Conexión AA
V105
92 x 10
h fondo viga + 2.00
h canto superior + 2.92
V105b
132 x 10
V116
20 x 82
h fondo viga + 2.50
h canto superior + 3.32
V111
10 x 92
h fondo viga + 2.00
h canto superior + 3.32
V112
10 x 82
PASE Ø 110
h centro=2,77
PASE Ø 15
V116
20 x 80
h fondo viga + 2.50
h canto superior + 3.32
CORTE DETALLE F-F
+3.32
+2.92
+2.69
+2.50

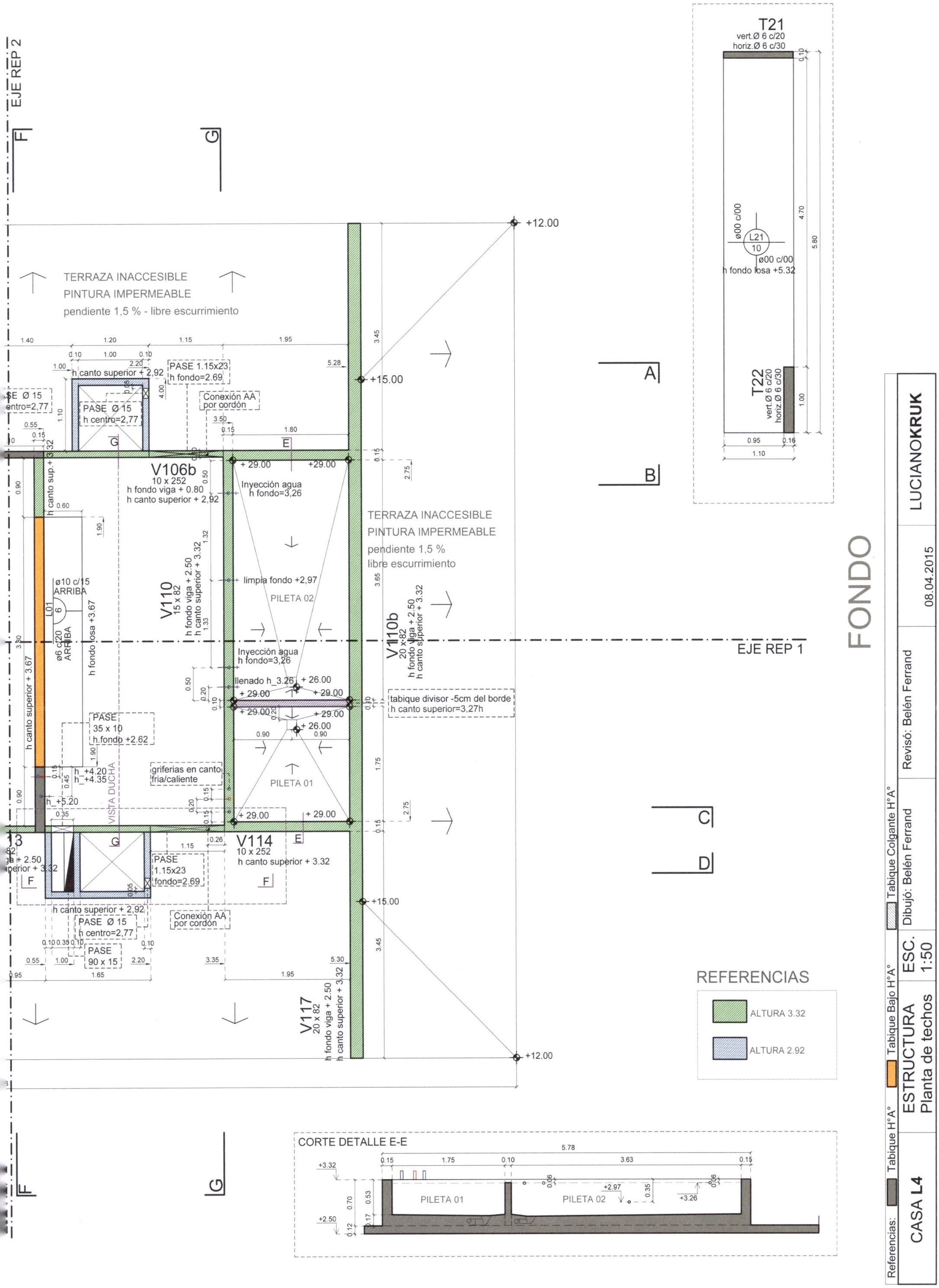

EJE REP 2
TERRAZA INACCESIBLE
PINTURA IMPERMEABLE
pendiente 1,5 % - libre escurrimiento
V106b
10 x 252
h fondo viga + 0.80
h canto superior + 2,92
V110
15 x 82
h fondo viga + 2.50
h canto superior + 3.32
V110b
20 x 82
V114
10 x 252
h canto superior + 3.32
V117
20 x 82
h fondo viga + 2.50
h canto superior + 3.32
Inyección agua
h fondo=3,26
limpia fondo +2,97
PILETA 02
PILETA 01
llenado h_3.26
tabique divisor -5cm del borde
h canto superior=3,27h
griferias en canto
fria/caliente
VISTA DUCHA
Conexión AA
por cordón
EJE REP 1
FONDO
T21
vert.Ø 6 c/20
horiz.Ø 6 c/30
T22
vert.Ø 6 c/20
horiz.Ø 6 c/30
h fondo losa +5.32
REFERENCIAS
ALTURA 3.32
ALTURA 2.92
CORTE DETALLE E-E
LUCIANOKRUK
08.04.2015
Revisó: Belén Ferrand
Dibujó: Belén Ferrand
ESC. 1:50
ESTRUCTURA
Planta de techos
CASA L4
Referencias: Tabique H°A° Tabique Bajo H°A° Tabique Colgante H°A°

>M2 de deck: 36m2

>Tablas Distancia de 1,3cm entre c/u

TABLAS

Medidas	Cantidad
2,50m	100
1,77m	25
0,77m	25

TIRANTES

Medidas	Cantidad
3" x 2" x 2.67m	25
1" x 2" x 2.8	1
1" x 2" x 0.13m	25

TACOS

Medidas	Cantidad
2" x 2" x 2cm	100

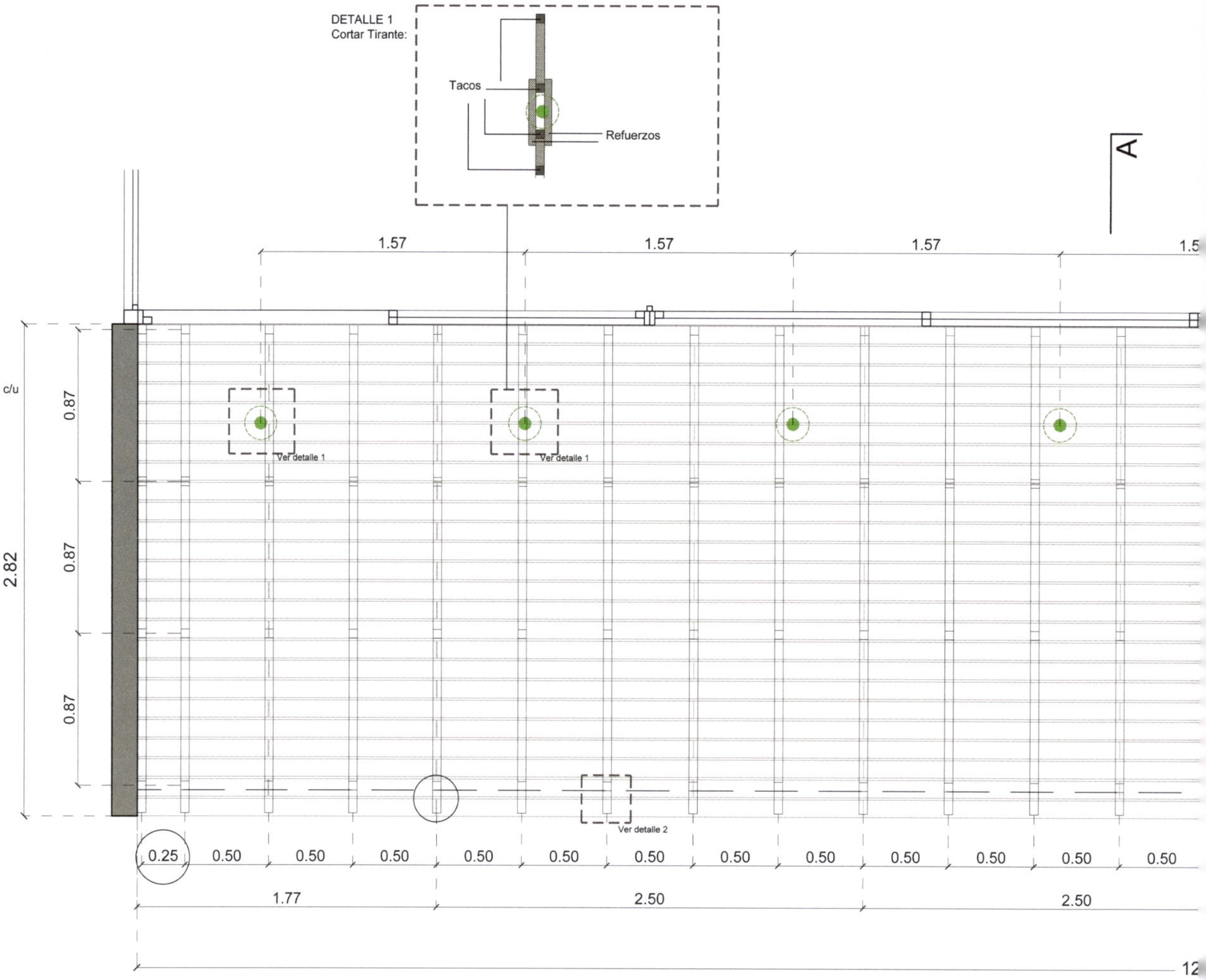

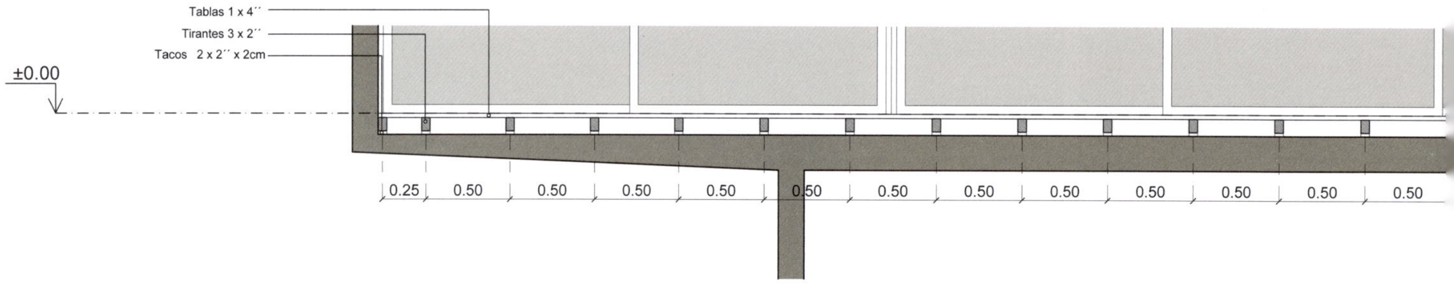

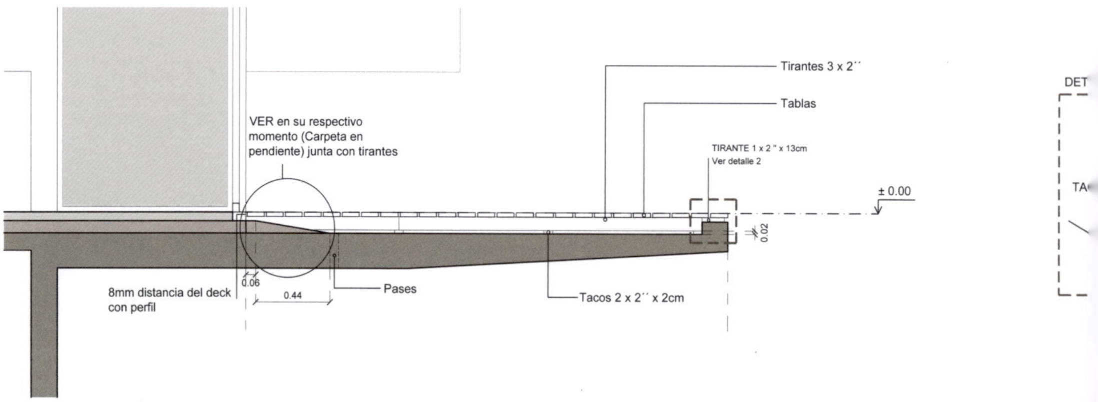

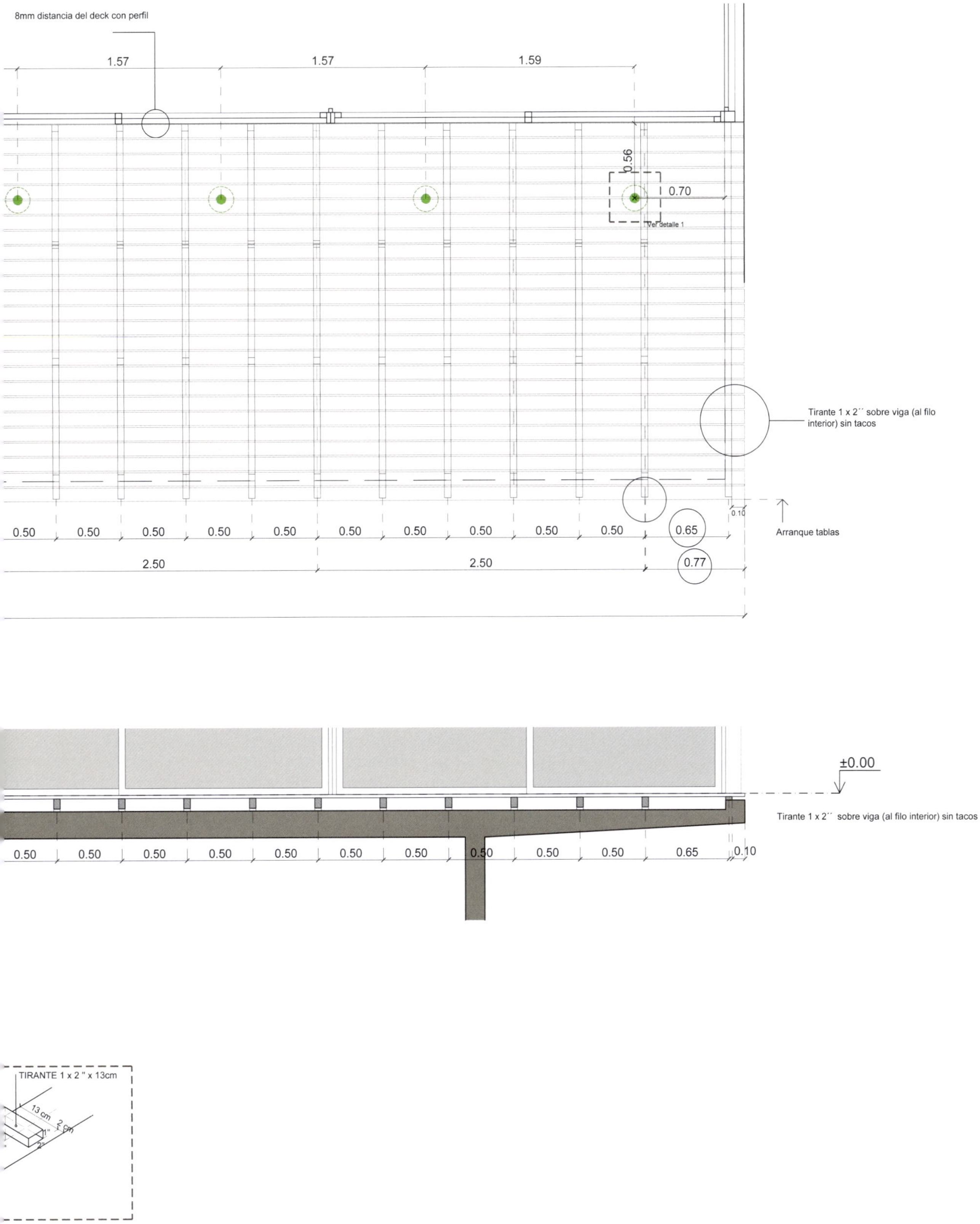

CASA **L4** | DECK PLANTA BAJA | ESC. 1:20 | Dibujó: Dan Saragusti | Revisó: Pablo Magdalena | 05/08/2015 | LUCIANO**KRUK**

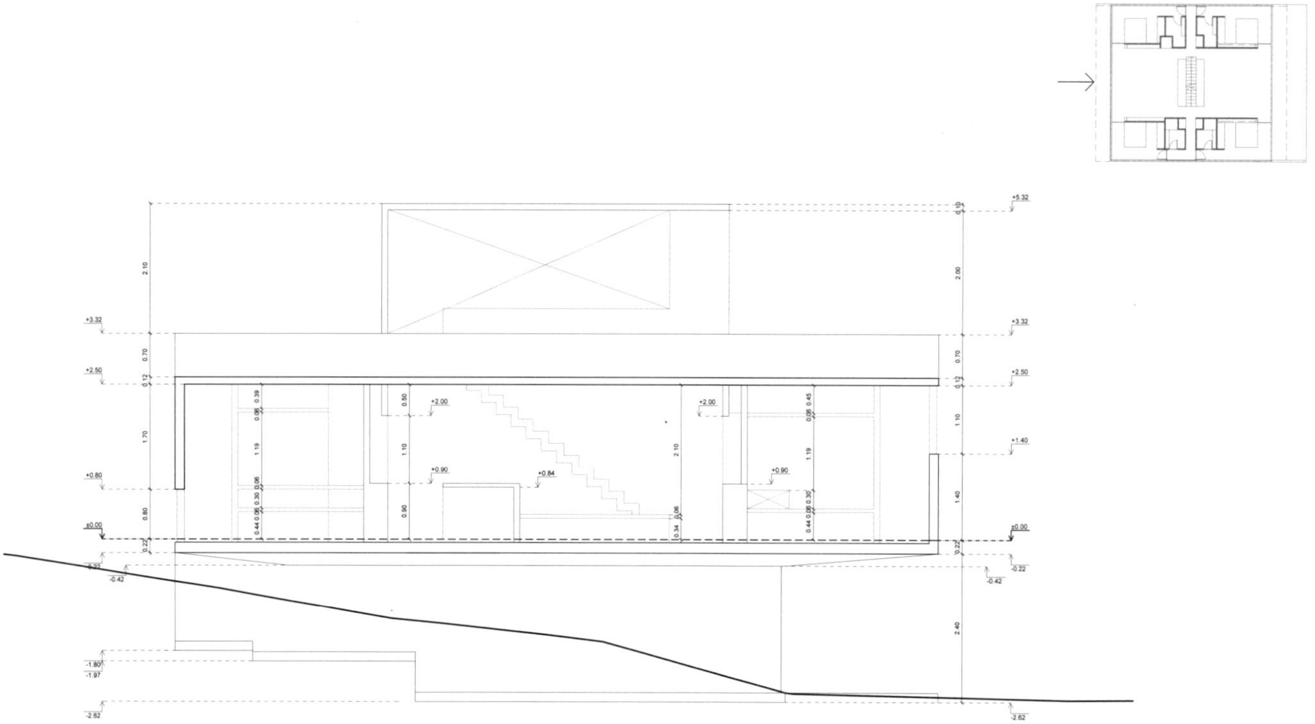

VISTA FRENTE

CASA **L4** | ESTRUCTURA VISTA FRENTE | ESC. 1:50 | Dibujó: Isabelle Ducrest | Revisó: Josefina P.S. | LUCIANO**KRUK**

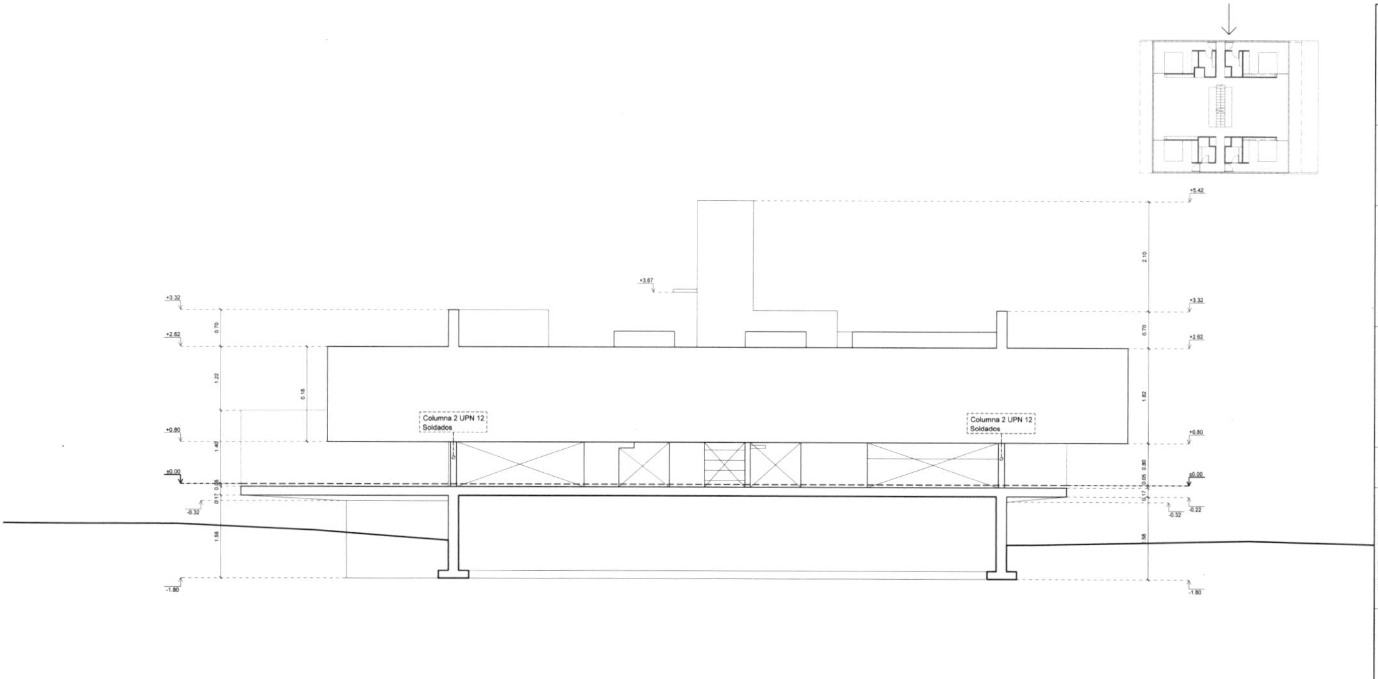

VISTA LATERAL IZQUIERDO

CASA **L4** | ESTRUCTURA VISTA LAT. IZQ. | ESC. 1:50 | Dibujó: Isabelle Ducrest | Revisó: Josefina P.S. | LUCIANO**KRUK**

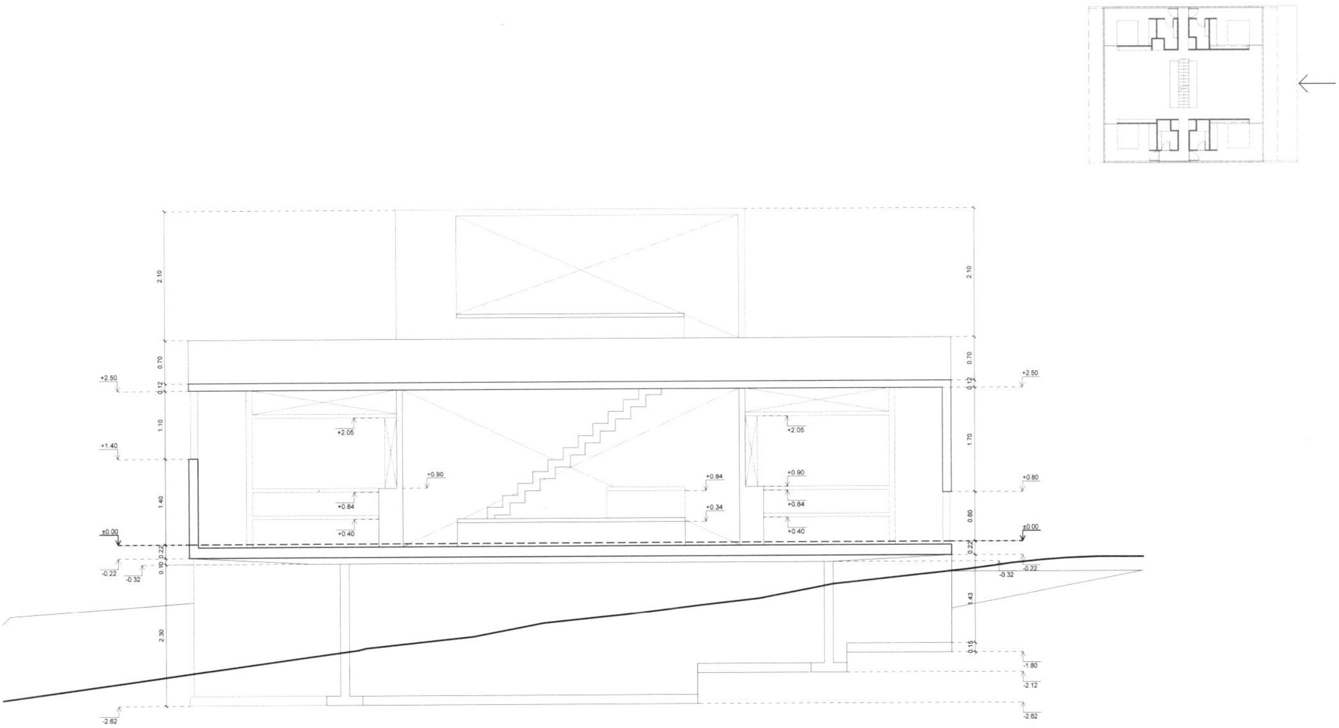

VISTA CONTRAFRENTE

CASA **L4** | ESTRUCTURA VISTA CONTRAF. | ESC. 1:50 | Dibujó: Isabelle Ducrest | Revisó: Josefina P.S. | LUCIANO**KRUK**

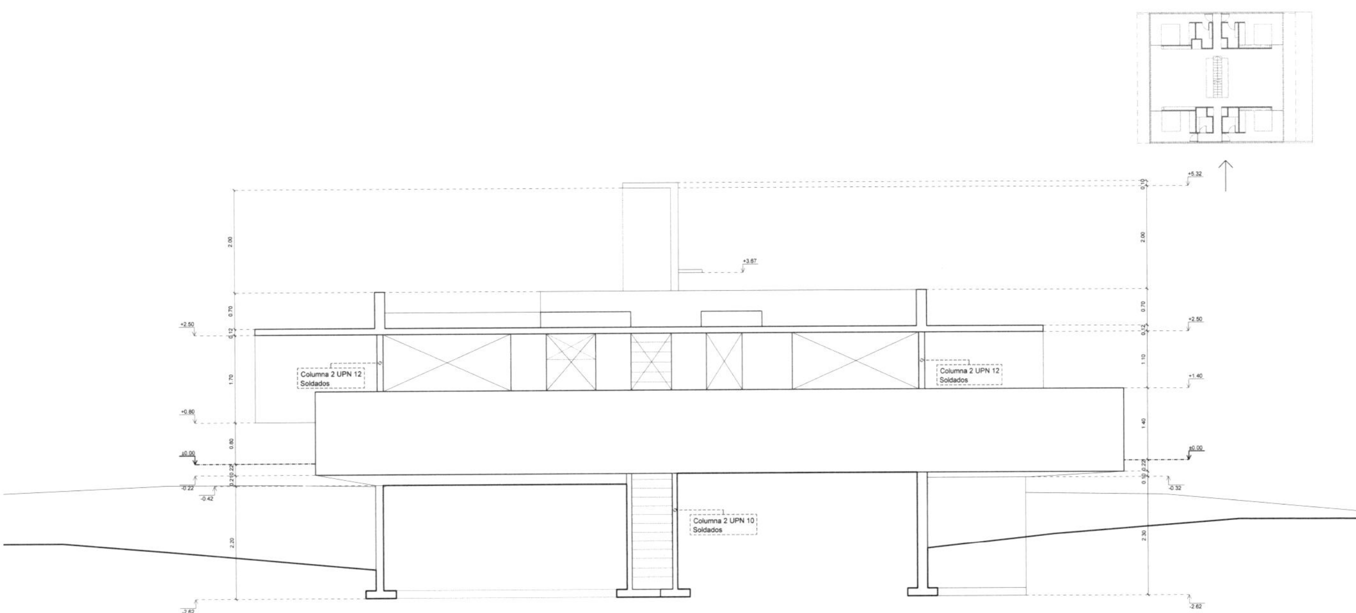

VISTA LATERAL DERECHO

CASA **L4** | ESTRUCTURA VISTA LAT. DER. | ESC. 1:50 | Dibujó: Isabelle Ducrest | Revisó: Josefina P.S. | LUCIANO**KRUK**

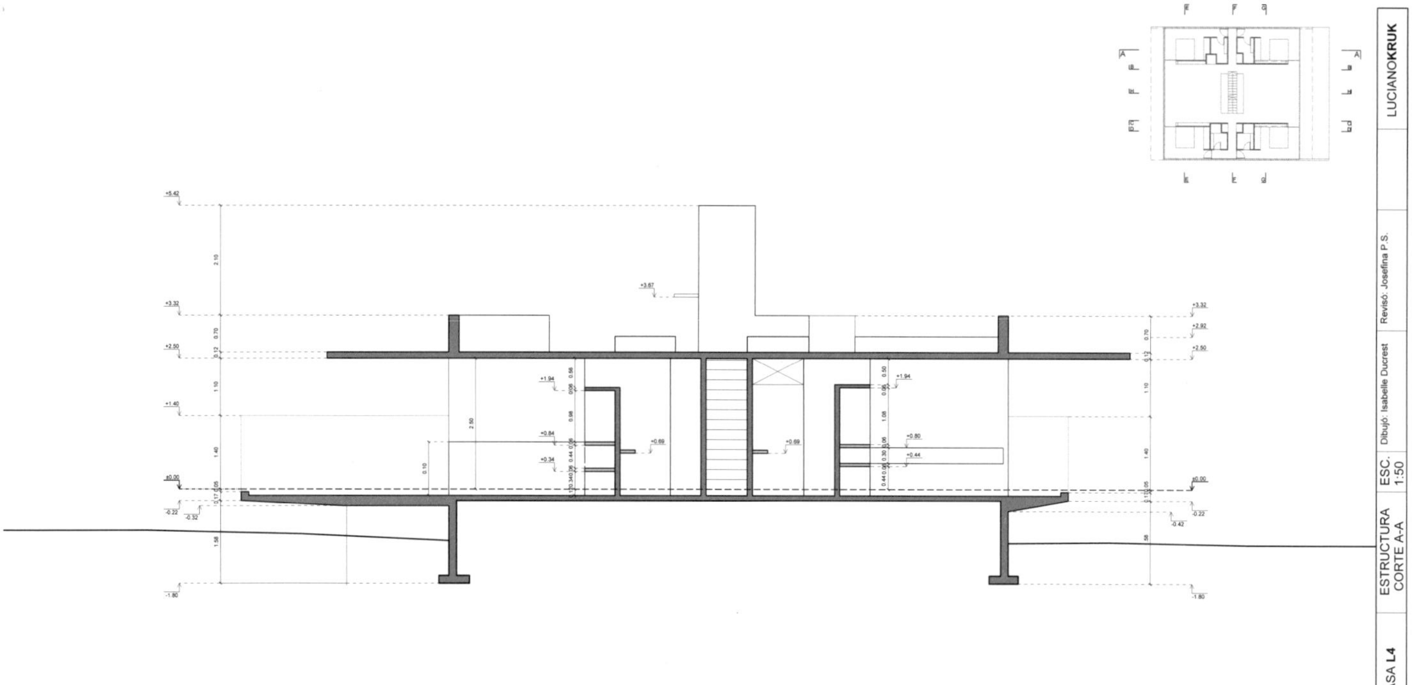

CORTE A

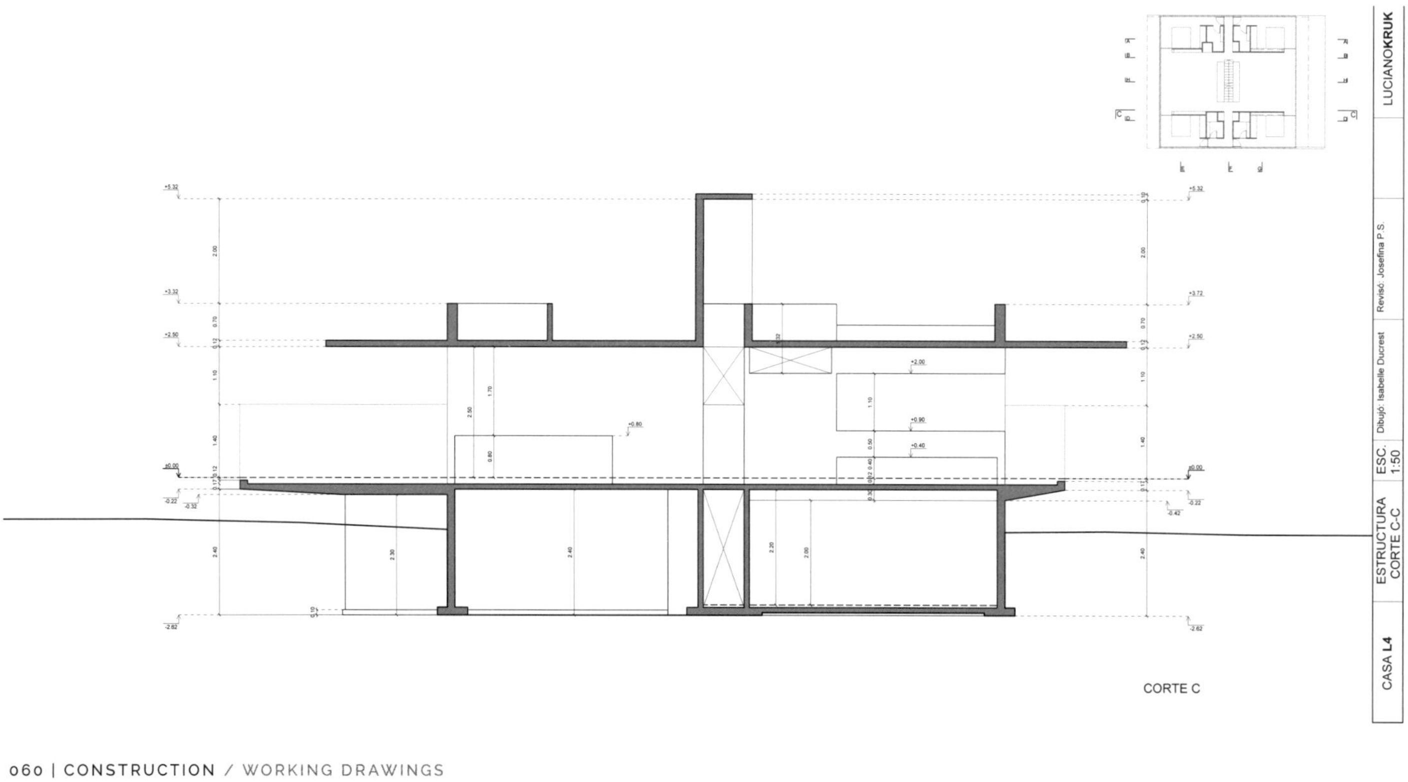

CORTE C

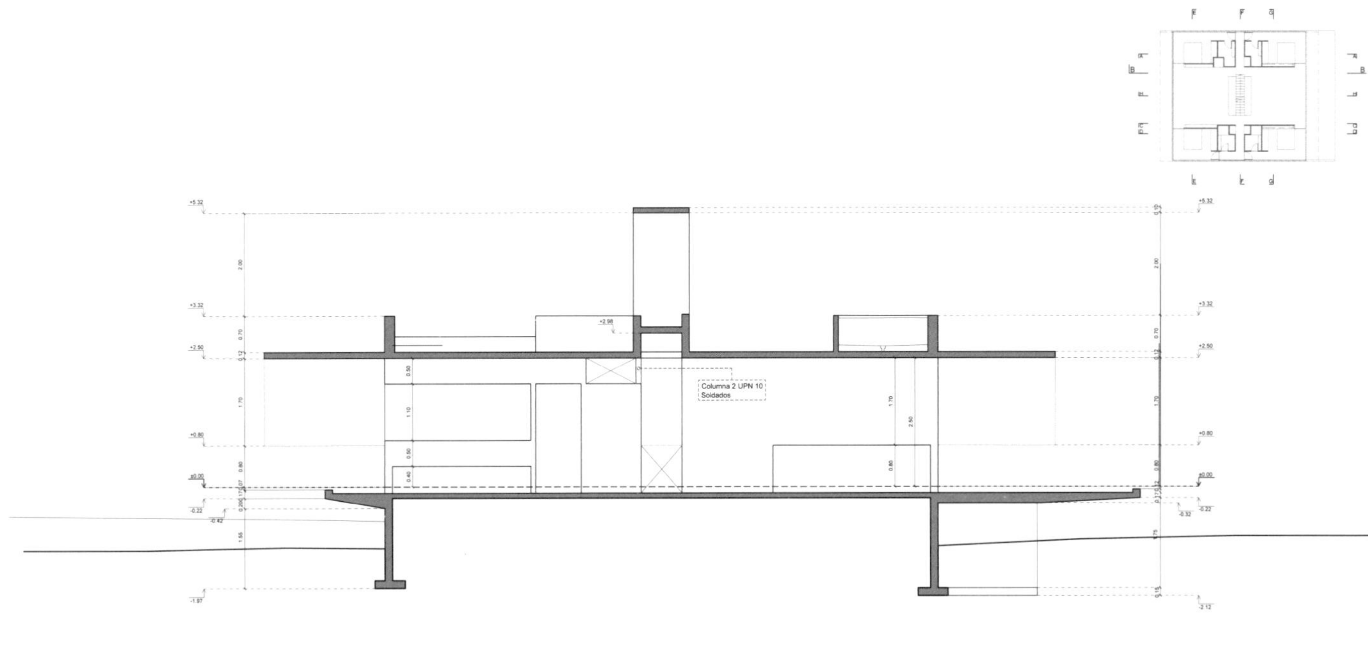

CORTE B

LUCIANOKRUK | Revisó: Josefina P.S. | Dibujó: Isabelle Ducrest | ESC. 1:50 | ESTRUCTURA CORTE B-B | CASA L4

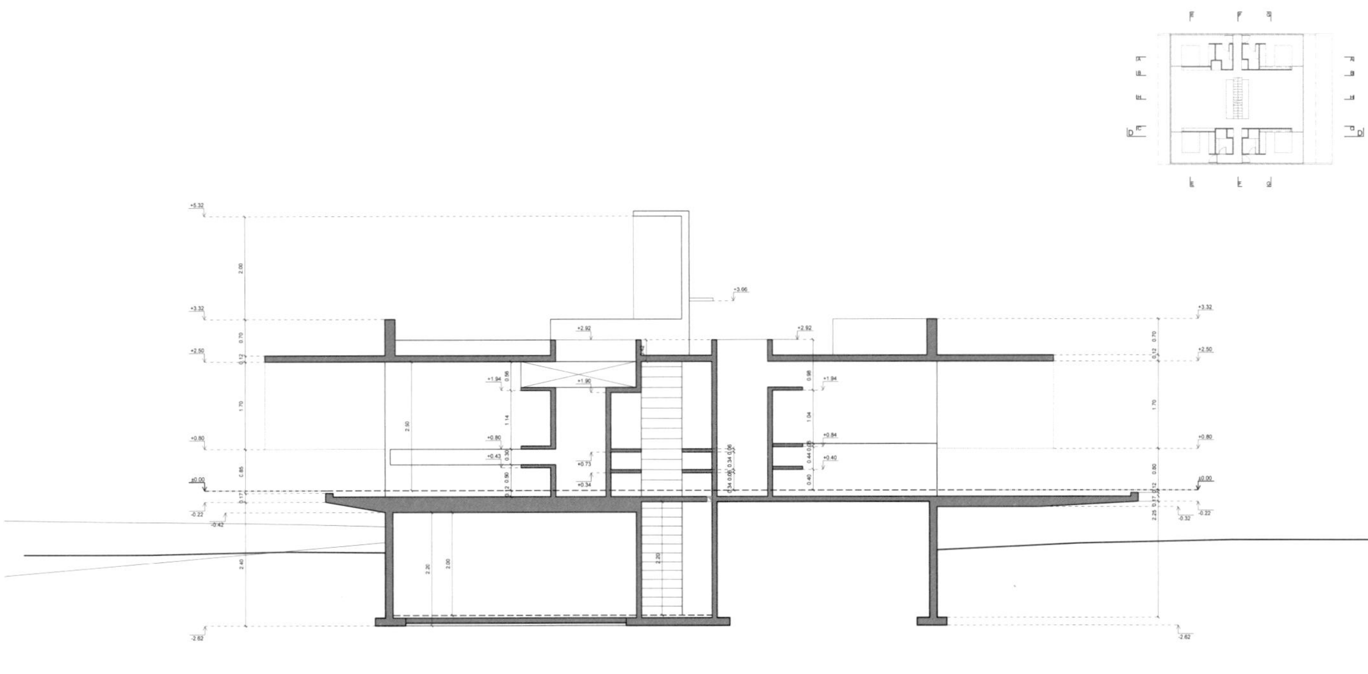

CORTE D

LUCIANOKRUK | Revisó: Josefina P.S. | Dibujó: Isabelle Ducrest | ESC. 1:50 | ESTRUCTURA CORTE D-D | CASA L4

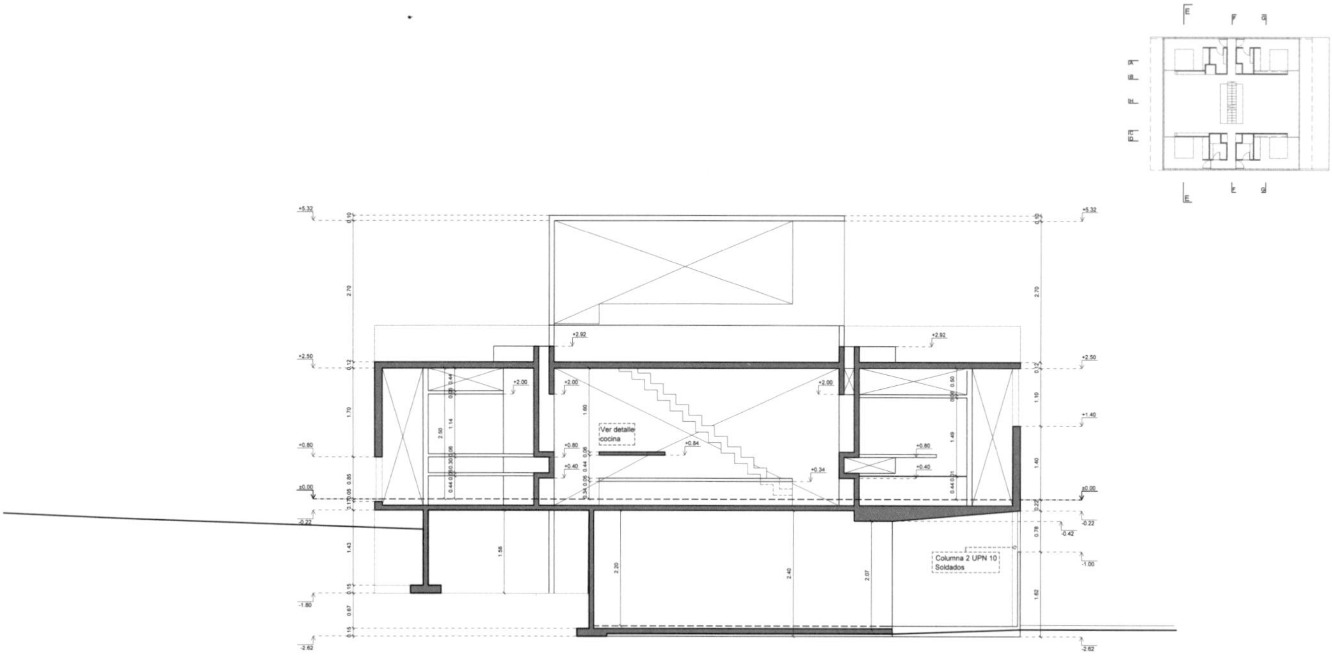

CORTE E

CASA L4 | ESTRUCTURA CORTE E-E | ESC. 1:50 | Dibujó: Isabelle Ducrest | Revisó: Josefina P.S. | LUCIANOKRUK

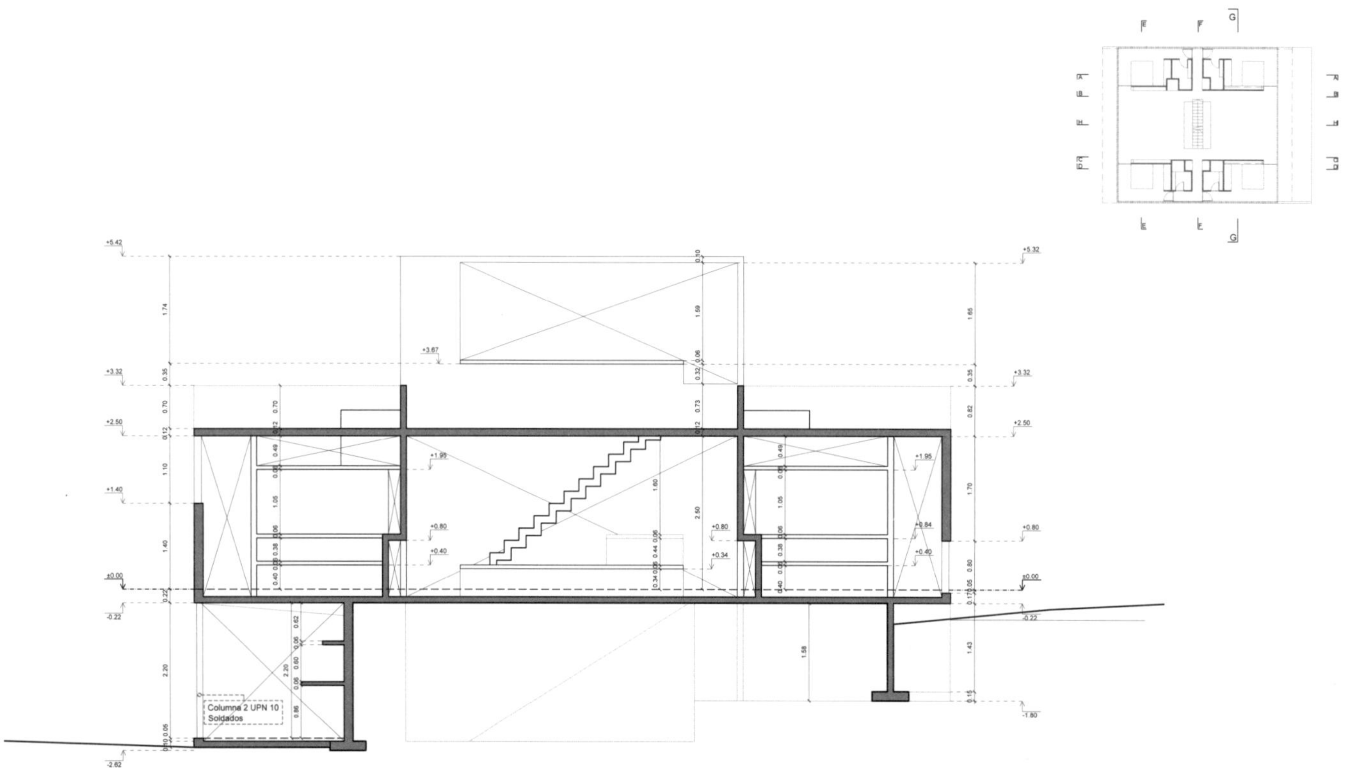

CORTE G

CASA L4 | ESTRUCTURA CORTE G-G | ESC. 1:50 | Dibujó: Isabelle Ducrest | Revisó: Josefina P.S. | LUCIANOKRUK

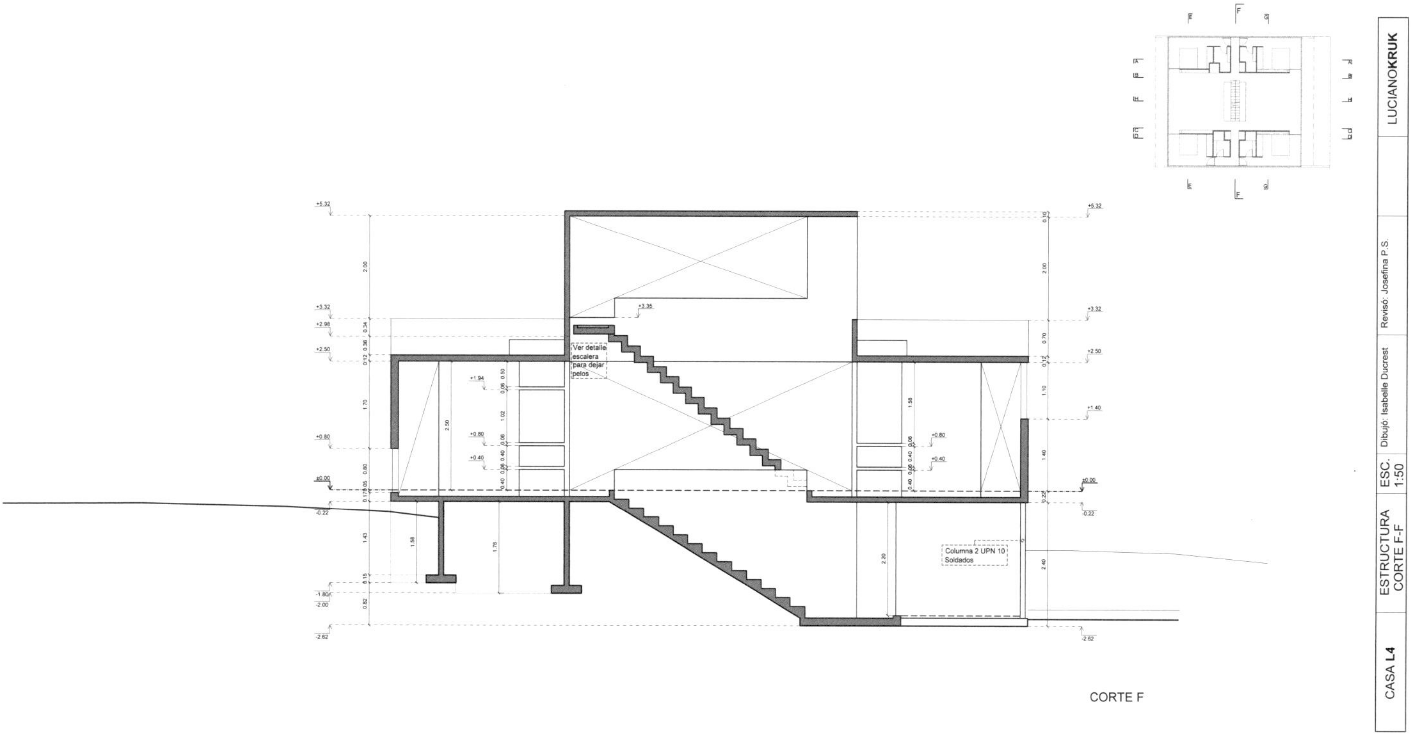

CORTE F

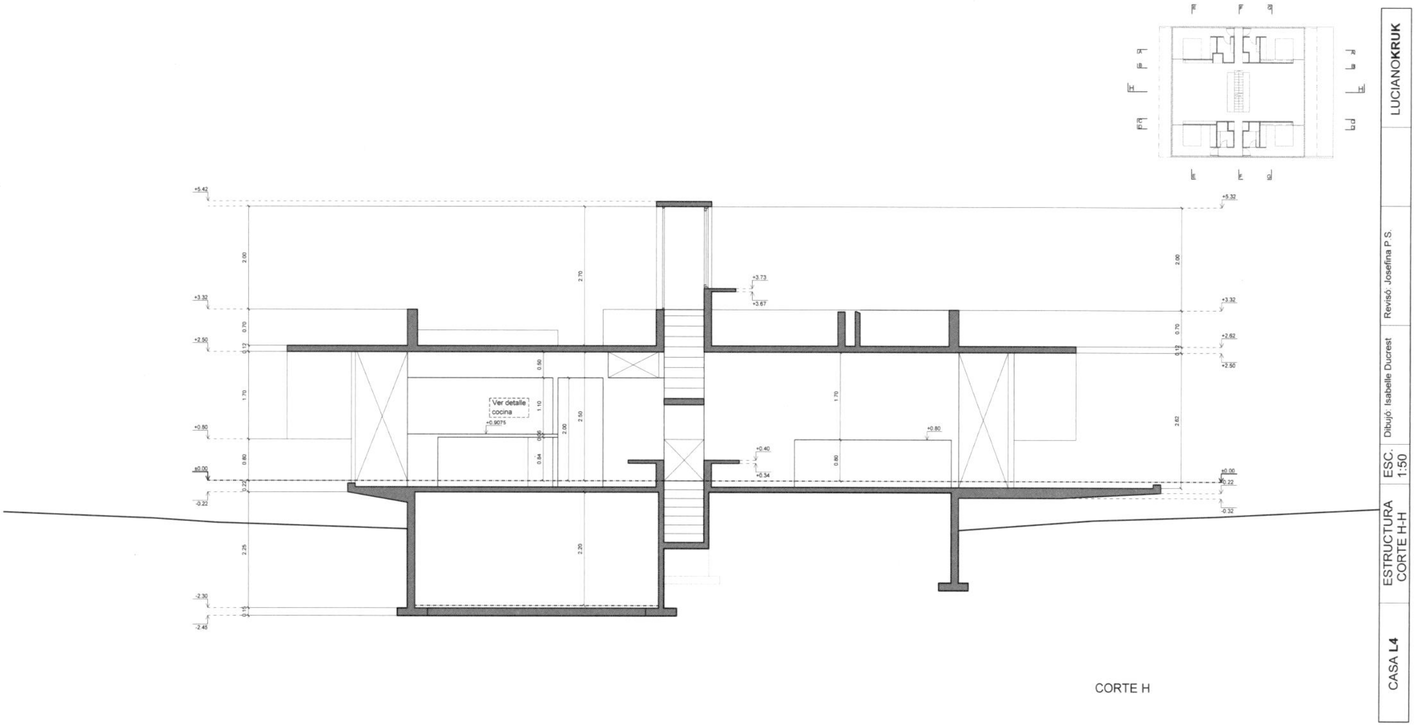

CORTE H

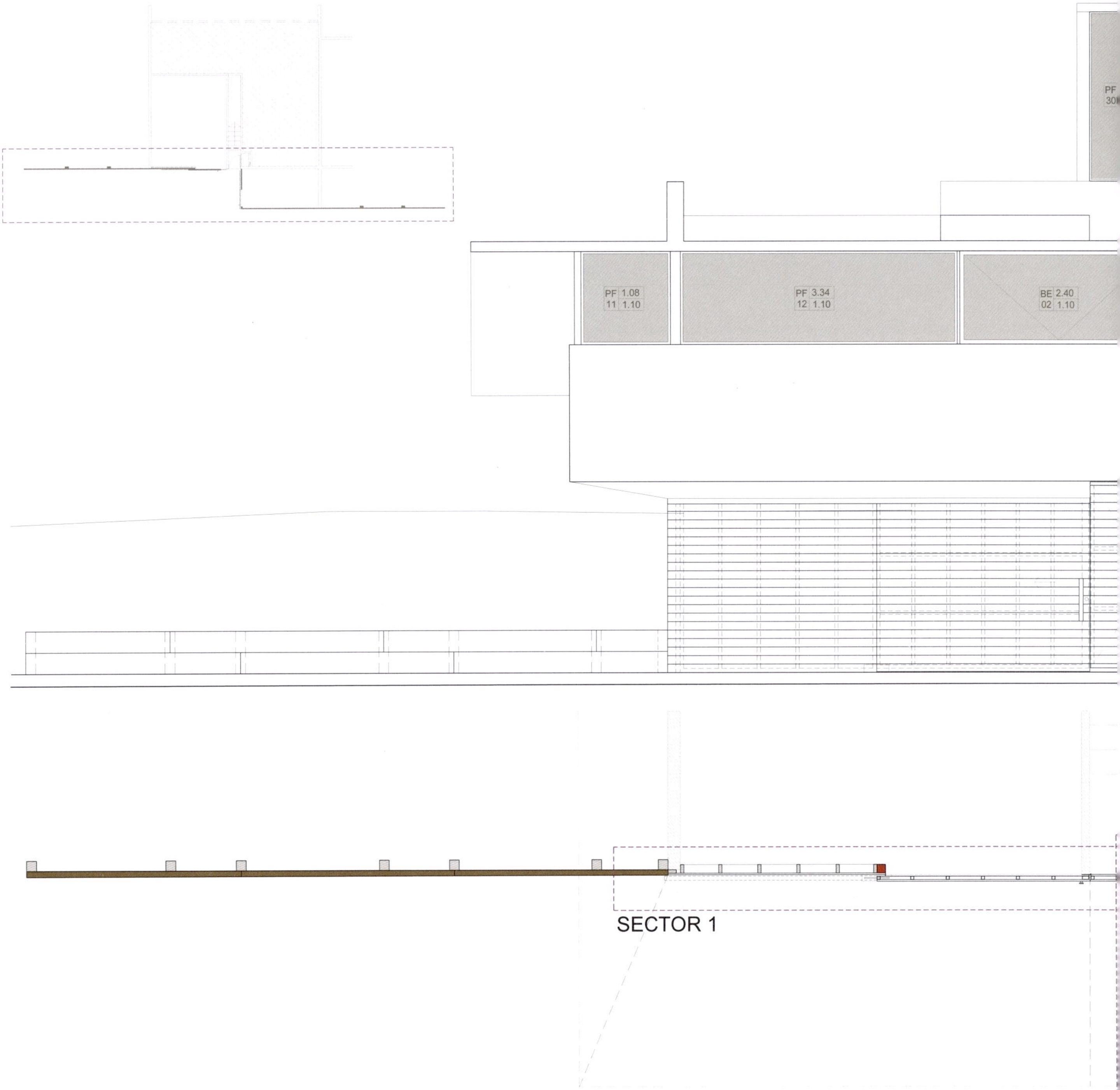
PF 1.08
11 1.10
PF 3.34
12 1.10
BE 2.40
02 1.10
SECTOR 1

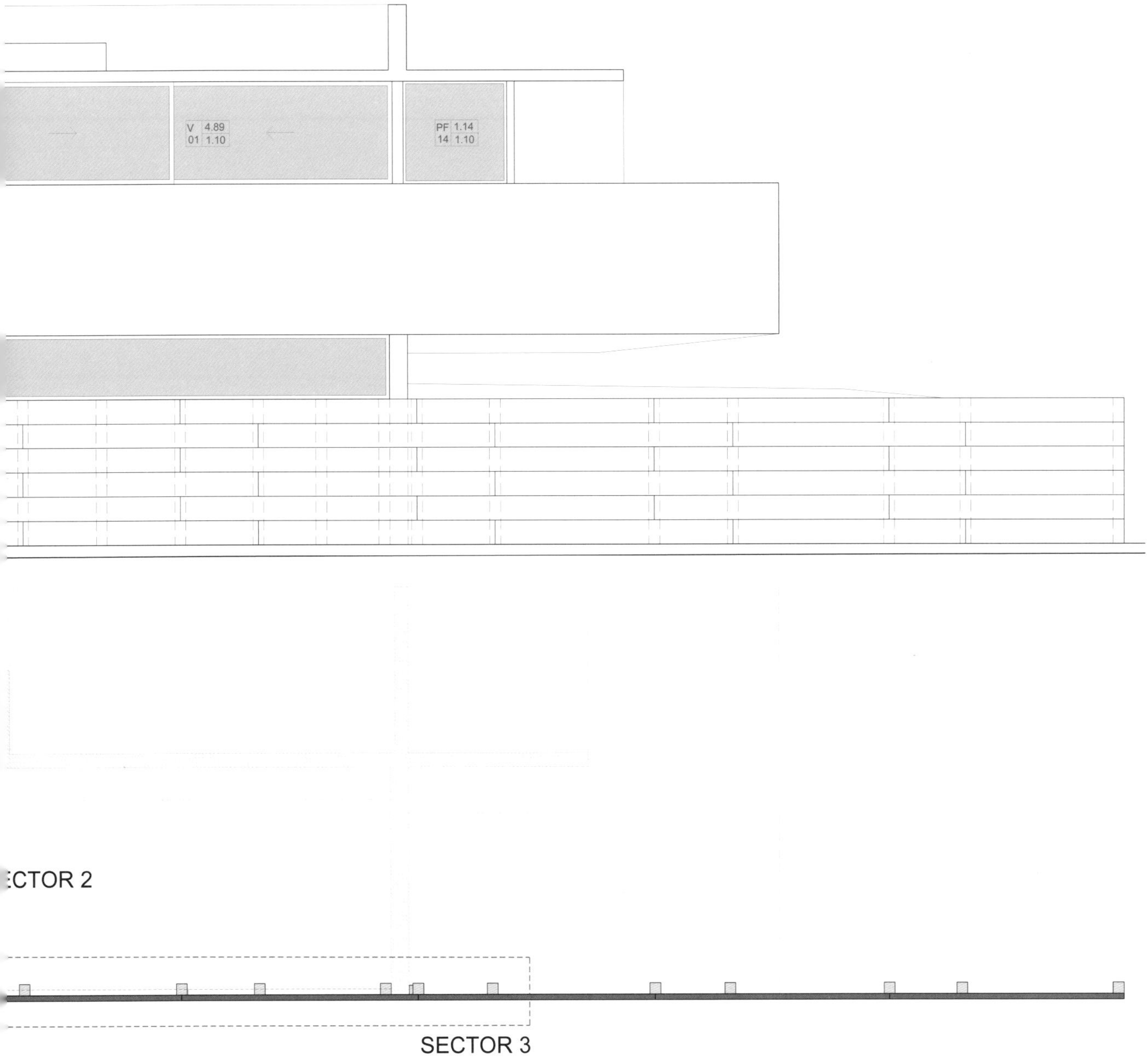

CASA **L4** | ARQUITECTURA - CERRAMIENTO MADERA LAT. DERECHO | ESC. 1:50 | Dibujó: Denise Andreoli | Revisó: Belén Ferrand | 01.07.2015 | LUCIANO**KRUK**

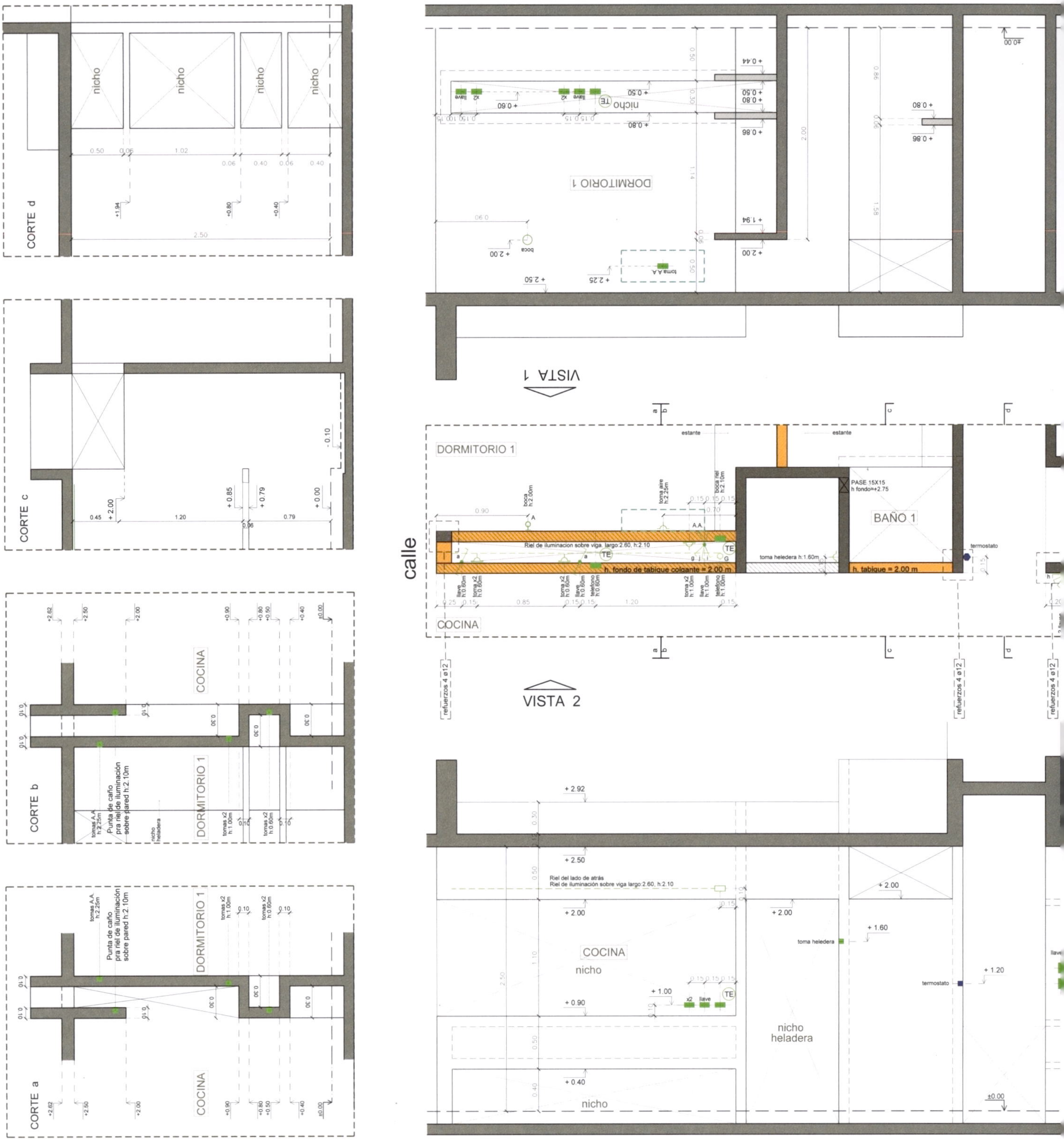

CORTE d
nicho
CORTE c
CORTE b
COCINA
DORMITORIO 1
CORTE a
DORMITORIO 1
VISTA 1
calle
BAÑO 1
COCINA
VISTA 2
nicho
nicho heladera

CASA **L4**	TABIQUE IZQ.	ESC. 1:20	Dibujó: Christian Studer	Revisó: Josefina P.S.	LUCIANO**KRUK**

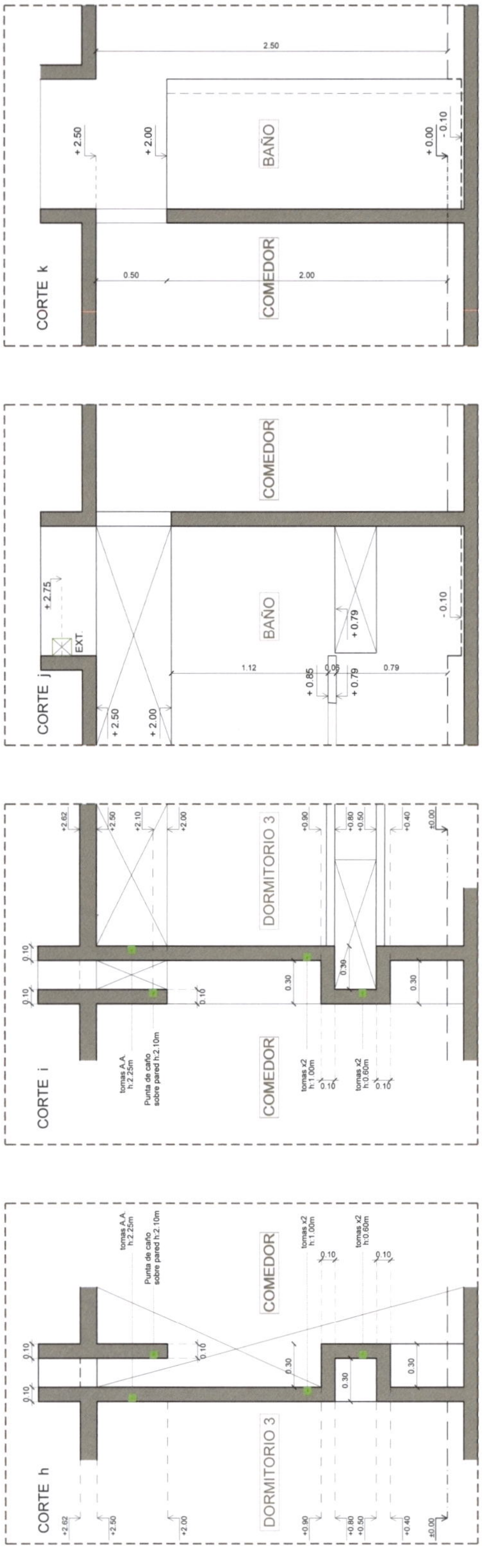

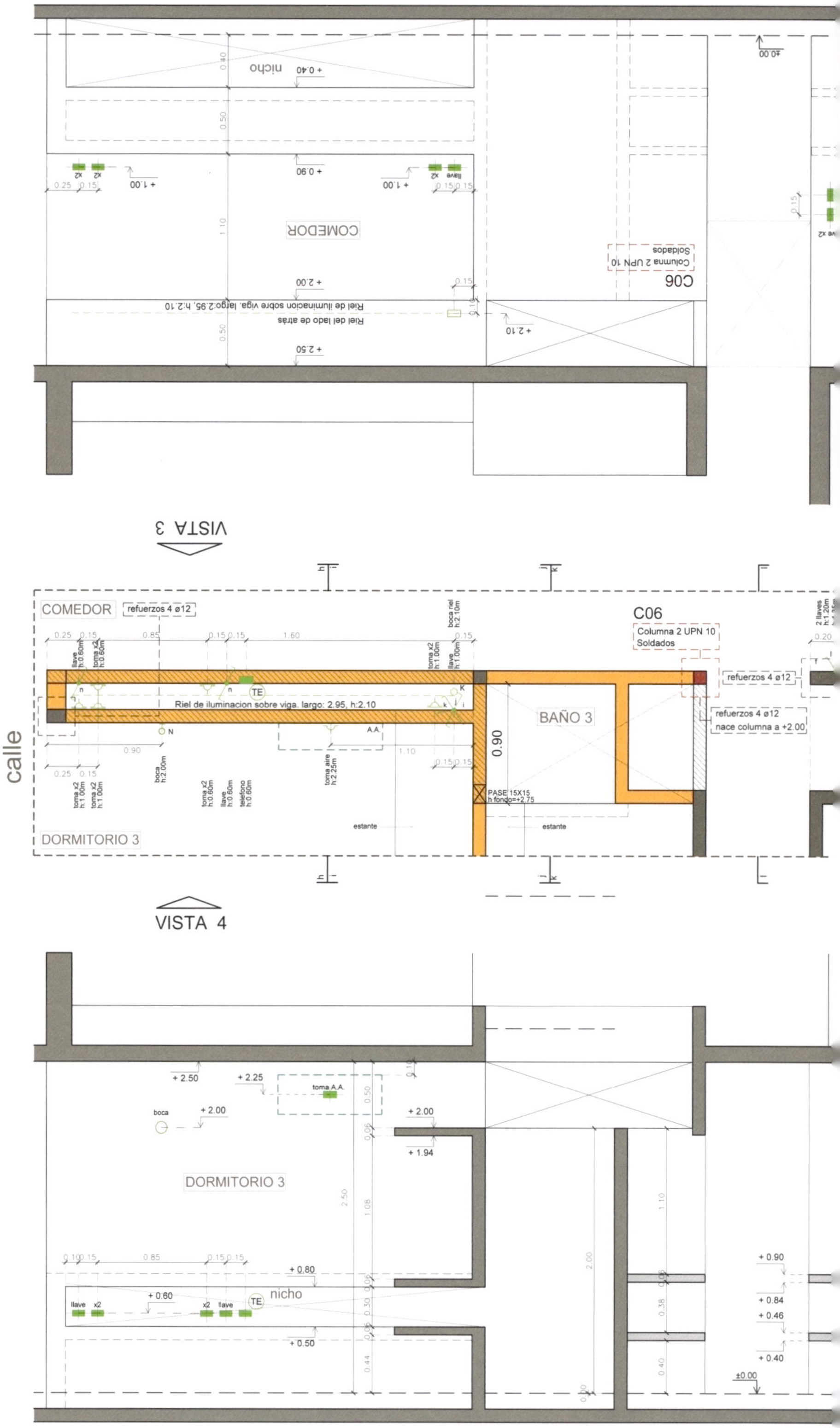

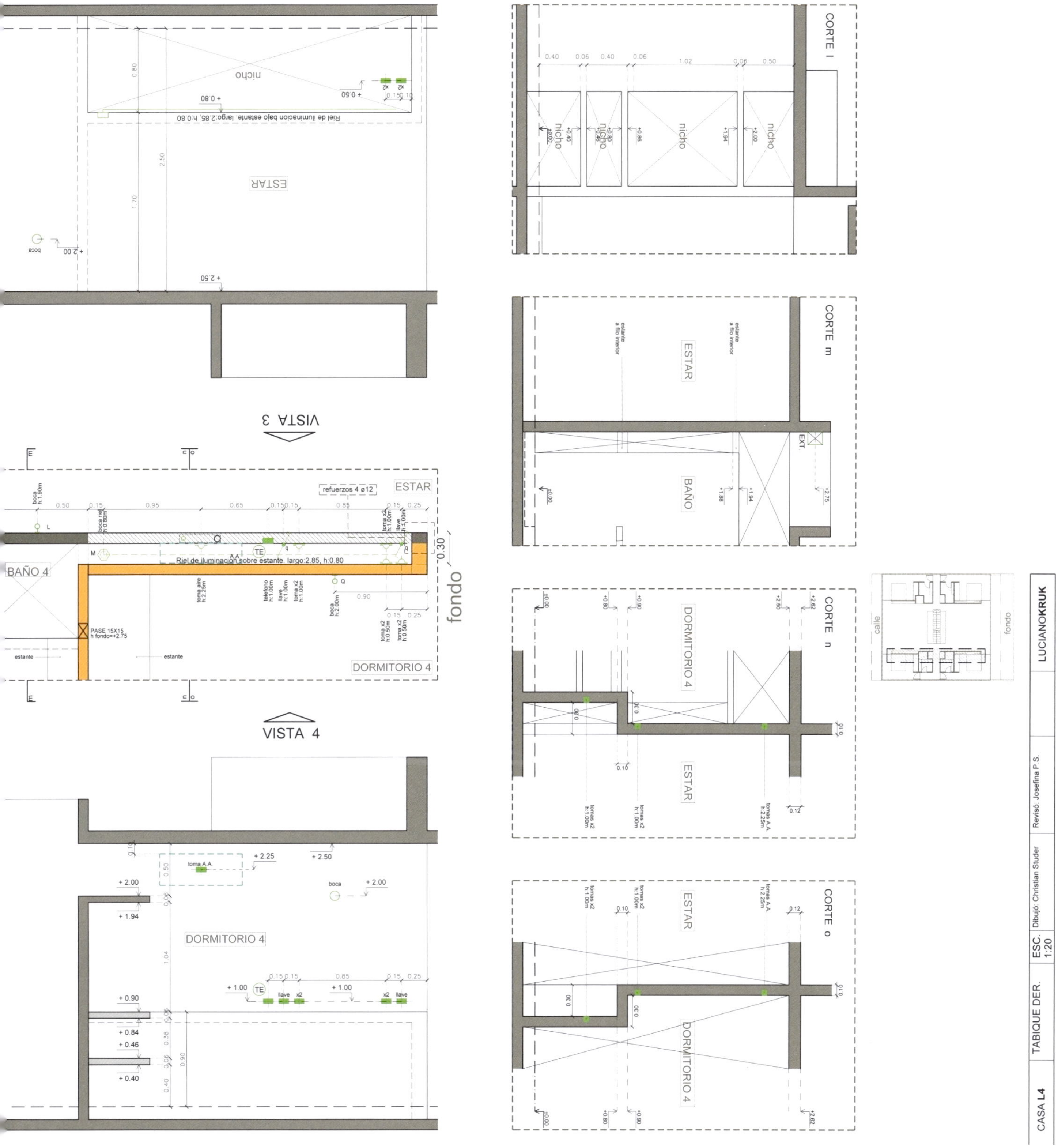

VISTA 3
VISTA 4
ESTAR
nicho
Riel de iluminación bajo estante. largo 2.85, h:0.80
BAÑO 4
DORMITORIO 4
refuerzos 4 ø12
Riel de iluminación sobre estante. largo 2.85, h:0.80
PASE 15X15
h fondo=+2.75
fondo
estante
toma A.A.
boca
CORTE l
CORTE m
CORTE n
CORTE o
BAÑO
EXT
calle
CASA L4
TABIQUE DER.
ESC. 1:20
Dibujó: Christian Studer
Revisó: Josefina P. S.
LUCIANOKRUK

SITE

PROCESS

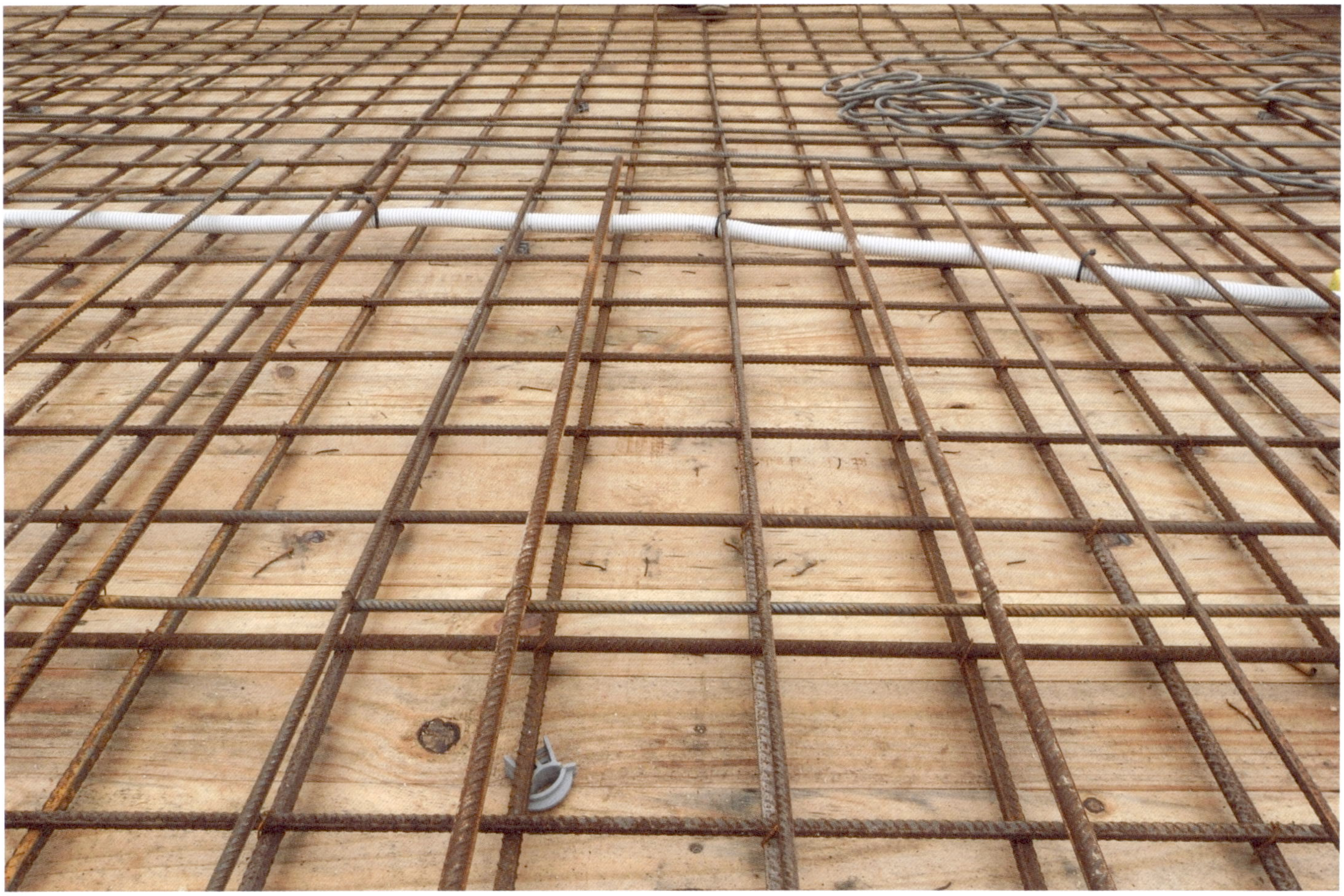

THE BUILDING

EPILOGUE

BY EKATERINA KUNZEL

"The moment we met I realized your work was like a dream worthy of its dreamer.

Authenticity in all its senses, that's your work's and your life's essence. It is the need not to hide anything, to be what you are; it is striving to be as good as you can. It is not lying, not hiding; it is exposing the structure, the reasoning, the poetry, the soul...

In your work, you showed that things can be done well and that the professionalism and the passion shown in the process persist afterwards in every corner, in every fragment, in every texture."

I think these words, from my first letter to Luciano, became as real as they could in this house, our house, our place in the world.

APPENDIX

BIOGRAPHY

Luciano Kruk was born on July 20, 1974, in Buenos Aires and in 2000 got a degree in Architecture at the University of Buenos Aires, where he taught Project until 2009. Nowadays, he continues to develop his academic activity as Visiting Professor. As such, he has been invited by the Superior Technical School of Architecture of Madrid (ETSAM-UPM); Iuav University of Venice; UNIVALI of Santa Catarina, in Brazil; USJT of São Paulo, in Brazil; and the Argentinian universities of San Martín (USAM), of Congreso (UC), in Mendoza, and of San Juan (UNSJ), where he conducted a post-graduate seminar. He has also given seminars and lectures at different conference series in Argentina, Brazil, Mexico, Spain and Italy.

He is a member of the architectural advisory committee at the National Commission of University Assessment and Accreditation (CONEAU). He is also a member of the Jury of the Province of Buenos Aires Association of Architects (CAPBA) and has participated as evaluator in the 2013.

Between 2000 and 2012, Luciano was a partner at BAKarquitectos architecture office (Besonías-Almeida-Kruk), where his work gained much recognition: among other awards, he received First Prize for Individual Housing Project at the 2007 and 2009 Biennials held by CAPBA; the Special Prize Eduardo Sacrite presented by CAPBA in 2005; First Prize from Alucobond for Young Architecture in 2005; and the Great Prize at the CPAU/SCA Biennial in 2006.

In 2012 he founded Luciano Kruk arquitectos architectural office, where he has been carrying out numerous individual and collective housing projects.

In 2015, Luciano was chosen as a representative for Argentina in the 9th International Festival of Architecture and Urbanism "Architecture Week Prague 2015", which took place in Prague, Check Republic.

His works have been published in numerous specialized media both in Argentina and abroad, in different countries in the Americas, Europe and Asia.

He has been invited as professor at the following universities:
-Superior Technical School of Architecture of Madrid, ETSAM, Madrid, Spain, 2016.
-Iuav University of Venice, Workshop WAVE Cicle, Venice, Italy, 2012.
-Universidade São Judas Tadeu, USJT, São Paulo, Brazil, 2011.
-National University of San Juan, San Juan, Argentina, 2013.
-University Univalí, Santa Catarina, Brazil, 2014.
-University of San Martin, San Martin, Argentina, 2015.

He has lectured in the following cycles:
- Design Patagonia, Museo Nacional de Bellas Artes, Neuquén, Argentina, 2007.
- Lecture Series, Professional Council of Architecture and Urbanism of Buenos Aires, Buenos Aires, Argentina, 2007.
- Pos seminar graduation Universidade São Judas Tadeu, USJT, São Paulo, Brazil, 2011.
- International Architecture Congress ARQEX, Merida, Mexico, 2014.
- International Congress of Architecture, Mendoza, Argentina, 2015.

Outstanding Awards:
- Single Dwelling First Prize for Franz House. SCA "Sociedad Central de Arquitectos", Buenos Aires, Argentina, 2012.
- Bienal of Architecture and Urbanism, Teory and Research Second Prize for JD House. Buenos Aires Province Chamber of Architects, Buenos Aires, Argentina, 2011.
- Architecture Award ARQ Argentina, Mention in the category Smaller Scale for House Cher. Buenos Aires, Argentina, 2011.
- Prize for Architecture, Planning, Research and Theory for "Beach House". Buenos Aires Province Chamber of Architects, Buenos Aires, Argentina, 2009.
- Competition "Architecture and Brick", Second Prize for "Brick House. XII Buenos Aires International Biennial of Architecture (XII BA09), Buenos Aires, Argentina, 2009.
-Third Honorable Mention for Concrete House. XVI BAQ Arqutecture Biennial, Pan Quito, Ecuador, 2008.
- First Biennial Prize for Architecture Planning, Research and Theory for Concrete House. Buenos Aires Province Chamber of Architects, Buenos Aires, Argentina, 2007.
- Grand Prix Biennial CPAU / SCA for "House Blue Sea". Central Society of Architects / Professional Council of Architecture and Urbanism, Buenos Aires, Argentina, 2006.
- Sacriste Award, Architecture, Planning, Research and Theory Biennale for "House Blue Sea". Buenos Aires Province Chamber of Architects, Buenos Aires, Argentina, 2005.
- First Young Architecture Prize, organized by Alucobond, 2005.

Outstanding exhibitions::
-The 9th Festival of Architecture and Urbanism, Prague, Czech Republic. September 2015.
- Recent Argentina Work Display, COAM Foundation (Colegio Oficial Arquitectos Madrid), Madrid, Spain. Concrete House. January 2011.
- XVII Quito Pan American Biennial of Architecture, Quito, Ecuador. "Beach House" and "US Building". November 2010.
- Biennial Prize SCA / CPAU (Central Society of Architects / Professional Council of Architecture and Urbanism), Malba Museum, Buenos Aires, Argentina. "Beach House", "US Building". October 2010.
- IV International Biennial of Architecture and Urbanism "Habitat + Inclusion". Museum Complex of the City of Lujan. November 2009.
- XII Buenos Aires International Biennial of Architecture, Buenos Aires, Argentina (XII BA09). "Building US", and "Blue Sea". September 2009.
- XII Congress Arquisur, Mar del Plata National University, Faculty of Architecture, Planning and Design, Mar del Plata, Argentina. Concrete House, October 2008.
- 11th International Venice Biennale of Architecture, Venice, Italy. Concrete House. September–November 2008.
- XVI Quito Pan American Biennial of Architecture, Quito, Ecuador. Concrete House. November 2008.
- 7th São Paulo Architecture Biennale, São Paulo, Brazil. Concrete and Mar Azul Houses. December 2007.
- XI Buenos Aires International Biennial of Architecture (XI BA07), Buenos Aires, Argentina. Concrete, Mar Azul and Pilar Houses. September 2007.

PROJECT CREDITS

Architect
Luciano Kruk

Design Team
Ekaterina Künzel, Architect
Luciano Kruk, Architect

Location
Costa Esmeralda, Buenos Aires, Argentina

Client
Luciano Kruk

Project
2015

Completion
2016

Land Area
1100 square meters

Built Area
185 square meters

Budget
US $800 / square meters

Site Manager
Pablo Magdalena

Collaborators
Josefina Perez Silva, Architect
Belén Ferrand, Architect
Andrés Conde Blanco, Architect
Leandro Rossi, Architect
Alberto Collet, Architect
Dan Saragusti
Giorgio Lorenzoli
Denise Andreoli
Federico Eichenberg

Text editing
Mariana Piqué, Architect

Photography
Daniela Mac Adden

Aerial photography
Diego Medina

Construction process photography
Ekaterina Kunzel

CONSTRUCTION

Structural system
Angel Fernandez

Roofing
Carlos Chaco Alvarez

Windows
Aberturas NIVEL, Ezequiel Vago, Martin Castiglione

Doors
La Grecca Home

Hardware
Herrajes de la Costa

Plumbing
Federico Eichenberg & Facundo Repetto

Woodwork and cabinetry
Marcos Klitzch

Sliding doors
Carlos Chaco Alvarez

Locksmithing
Herrajes de la Costa

Glasswork
Aberturas Nivel, Ezequiel Vago, Martin Castiglione

Painting
Carlos Chaco Alvarez

Electricity, heating and cooling
Raul Alfredo Gutierrez

Electrical systems
Raul Alfredo Gutierrez

Lighting design
Ekaterina Kunzel

Plumbing system
Federico Eichenberg & Facundo Repetto

Plumbing fixtures
Ferrum - FV

Bathroom fixtures
Ferrum - FV

Swimming pool
Federico Eichenberg & Facundo Repetto

Kitchen installation
Marcos Klitzch

Roller blinds
Carolina Mateos

PHOTOGRAPHY CAPTIONS

Left side view.

Back deck view.

Aerial view towards the sea.

Construction process.
Slab shuttering.

Construction process.
Slab shuttering.

Construction process. Builder:
Ángel Fernandez.

Luciano Kruk with site manager
Federico Eichenberg.

Luciano Kruk with builder Ángel
Fernandez, site manager Federico
Eichenberg and project coordinator
Pablo Magdalena.

Right side detail view towards
the front.

View of the house from the woods.

Construction process. Roof slab
shuttering. Date: July 2015.

Construction process.
Slab shuttering.

Construction process.
Slab shuttering.

Construction process.
Slab shuttering.

Construction process. Roof slab
shuttering.

Construction process.
Slab shuttering.

Construction process.

Construction process.

Construction process. Shoring of slab shuttering.

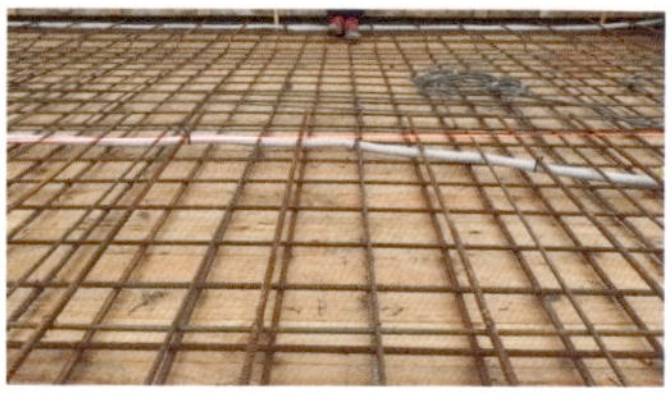

Construction process. Slab's steel reinforcement.

Construction process.

Construction process. Partitions shuttering.

Construction process. View from the bedrooms' inner hallway.

Construction process.

Construction process. Recent slab deshuttering.

Construction process. Recent slab deshuttering.

Construction process. Recent slab deshuttering.

Construction process. Recent slab deshuttering.

Construction process. Recent installation of aluminum framings and glazed panels.

Construction process. Glass panels installation between quebracho wood framings on the ground floor and the concrete partition.

Construction process. Final building adjustments.

Construction process. Final building adjustments.

Construction process. Final building adjustments. Finishing the quebracho wood deck towards the woods.

Construction process. Detail of the skylight in the kitchen.

Construction process. House's central staircase shuttering.

Construction process. House's central staircase deshuttering and final building adjustments.

Right side view.

View of the engine and the washing room at the lower part of the house.

Right side detail view towards the terrace at the rear.

View of the right corner and the terrace at the rear of the house.

Construction process. Dune's final leveling under the terrace.

Construction process. House's central staircase shuttering.

Construction process. House's central staircase recent deshuttering.

Aerial view towards Costa Esmeralda's shore.

View from the front right side of the house and the entrance under the wooden gates.

View from the front right side of the house and the entrance under the wooden gates.

View of the right corner and the terrace at the rear of the house.

View of the house or rear view of the house with terrace merging with the woods.

Rear view of the house from the woods.

Concrete table built in the woods at the back end of the site.

The house from the woods.

Left side view of the house.

Left side view of the house from the woods.

Left side view of the house towards the front.

Detail of the framings at the front of the house.

Front view of the house from its entrance path.

Rear view of the house from the woods.

Far view of the house from the woods.

Left side view of the house.

Side view of the house. Deck detail.

Left side view of the house.

View of the left front corner of the house.

View of the left front corner of the house.

Front view towards the corner where the entrance is, at the lower part of the house.

House entrance through the narrow stairs between two concrete doors.

View of the house's social areas and stairs standing out. The house's entrance facing downwards.

Picture of the living room merging towards the woods.

The social area catching the view from the living room on the foreground, the main stairs and the kitchen, the dining room and the landscape at the back.

The social area catching the view from the living room on the foreground, the main stairs and the kitchen, the dining room and the landscape at the back.

Detail of a rough concrete partition in the dining room area.

View from the kitchen and dining room areas looking towards the landscape beyond.

Detail of the kitchen counter on the foreground and the dining area at the back.

View from the living room towards the kitchen and dining room.

Picture of the center of the house which is its social area and the stairs stand out.

Picture of a corner of the living room.

View of the living room.

Detail of the dining room with light dripping from above through the concrete partitions.

Detail of the stairs and the island floating above the floor that functions as a cooking space.

View from the kitchen and dining room areas looking towards the living room and the landscape at the back.

Detail of the counter, especially designed for this house, made of iron profiles and quebracho planks.

Picture showing how the social area on the left merges with a bedroom on the right by means of a double glazed panel that provides acoustic isolation while a curtain gives privacy to the bedroom.

View of the bedroom on the left towards the rear of the house The horizontal window on the ground level under the concrete partition.

View of one of the bathrooms View of the shower with daylight dripping through an opening on the roof.

View of the bedroom towards the right side and the front of the house showing the high window above the partition.

View of the bedroom towards the rear of the house and towards the right side. Picture taken from the deck.

View of a concrete partition in the social area showing the effect of the light at a certain time of the day.

View of the social area taken from the kitchen-dining room space.

Detail of the main stairs of the house.

View of one of the front bedrooms, in which the concrete wall becomes the shelves behind the bed.

View of the bedroom on the left of the house towards the front.

View of the bedroom towards the right side and the front of the house showing how it merges with the glazed panels on the facade.

View of the bedroom towards the front of the house and towards the right side.

View of one of the bathrooms.

View of one of the bathrooms showing the glazed voids merging and giving continuity to the space.

Picture of the main stairs showing the opening towards the terrace.

View of the area on the roof with its small swimming pool and the wooden deck inviting to enjoy the surrounding woods.

View of the contemplative space on the roof taken from one of its sides.

View of the area on the roof with its small swimming pool and the wooden deck inviting to enjoy the surrounding woods.

Night view of the front of the house and the left side.

Night view of the front of the house.

View of the swimming pool on the roof and the woody landscape surrounding the house.

Night view of the house showing the entrance area.

The trace left by the construction machinery on the sand.

BOOK CREDITS

Book Layout by Oscar Riera Ojeda

OSCAR RIERA OJEDA
PUBLISHERS

ISBN 978-1-946226-01-3
Published by Oscar Riera Ojeda Publishers Limited
Printed in China

Oscar Riera Ojeda Publishers Limited
Unit 4-6, 7/F.,
Far East Consortium Building,
121 Des Voeux Road Central, Hong Kong
T: +852-5311-1625

Production Offices | China
Suit 19, Shenyun Road,
Nanshan District, Shenzhen 518055
T:+86-182-0098-3774

www.oropublishers.com | www.oscarrieraojeda.com
oscar@oscarrieraojeda.com